POCKET POSTERS

Why Pocket Posters?

Daydream Education, the UK's leading provider of educational posters, has developed a versatile range of colourful and engaging revision guides that break down barriers to learning and encourage independent study.

Small in size, huge in content!

Designed to engage learners, Pocket Posters are the perfect alternative to the larger text-heavy revision guides. The pocket-sized revision guides simplify key GCSE content into bitesize chunks of information to improve pupils' understanding and boost confidence.

Daydream Education | Unit 1 | Central Park | Western Avenue | Bridgend | CF31 3RH
Tel: 0844 800 1660 | Fax: 0844 800 1664 | www.daydreameducation.co.uk
Chris Malcolm Ltd. t/a Daydream Education. Registered in England and Wales. Company No: 04216204

GCSE Design & Technology

Contents

New & Emerging Technologies

Technology is transforming the world around us, impacting hugely on the environment and the way we live, work and communicate.

Enterprise

The use of new and emerging technologies has significantly transformed enterprise, presenting new and exciting opportunities for businesses and entrepreneurs.

Enterprise is the ability to identify business opportunities and take advantage of them. Successful businesses are those that are innovative and can adapt quickly to change. Being able to identify new and emerging technologies helps businesses generate new ideas.

Crowdfunding

Historically, to fund a new product or a new business venture, a bank loan or an investor was needed. Crowdfunding offers a new solution, enabling individuals or businesses to promote an idea on a platform, such as a website, to a large audience. People can then choose to invest money in the projects they like.

Backers are generally rewarded for their investment, usually in the form of a gift, discount or share in the business.

Virtual Marketing and Retailing

The increased use of the Internet has led to the rise of virtual marketing to reach a wider market. This includes online advertising, such as social media adverts and pay-per-click advertising, which involves businesses paying to appear prominently in search engine results.

Virtual retailing allows shoppers to buy products online. Most businesses now have online stores and websites where customers can shop.

Cooperatives

A cooperative is a business that is owned and run by its workers or members. The workers or members make the business decisions and share in the profits made.

Cooperatives are usually based around local communities, but they can also be large businesses, such as Nationwide Building Society.

Fair Trade

Fair trade ensures that farmers in lower-income countries get a fair price for their produce, so they can provide for their families. It also aims to improve trade terms and conditions for workers.

Fair trade items are labelled accordingly to help consumers make ethical buying choices.

daydream EDUCATION

The use of new and emerging technologies has significantly changed the way in which goods are manufactured.

Automation and Robotics

Automation involves the use of automatic equipment in manufacturing. It was first developed and used on a large scale during the Industrial Revolution to help meet increased demand for manufactured goods.

Although the initial cost of automated equipment is high, it can significantly improve productivity, enabling manufacturers to create high-quality products quickly and cheaply.

Industrial robots can be programmed to carry out various automated tasks, including welding, assembling parts, painting, labelling and packaging.

Advantages of Automation & Robotics

- Increased efficiency and productivity
- Fewer errors and greater accuracy
- Limited human input, reducing labour costs
- The ability to perform work that is otherwise dangerous for humans

Disadvantages of Automation & Robotics

- Expensive to set up and maintain
- Replaces human labour, leading to job losses
- No human judgement
- Requires high-skilled workers to operate the equipment

Buildings and Equipment

Technologies, such as Wi-Fi and 4G, have significantly improved workplace efficiency by enabling faster communication and data transfer and greater workforce mobility. New technologies have also led to greater energy efficiency in buildings and equipment.

Computer-Aided Design & Computer-Aided Manufacture

Computer aided design (CAD) and computer aided manufacture (CAM) are used to design and manufacture products. Both have helped in the transition from product design to product manufacture and have greatly affected workplace efficiency.

CAD allows users to draw, design and model products using specialist software. Designers can create both 2D and 3D models and manipulate their designs to test different ideas before manufacture.

Examples of CAD software: AutoCAD, SolidWorks, Autodesk Inventor and 2D Design

CAM uses computer numerical control (CNC) to create CAD designs. The CAD software creates the 3D coordinates of every point of the design, and the CAM machine then interprets the coordinates to manufacture the design.

Examples of CAM equipment: laser cutters, 3D printers, CNC routers and CNC lathes

Advantages of CAD

- More accurate than hand drawings
- Enables designs to be extensively amended and tested before production
- Allows several designers to work on the same project simultaneously
- Offers views of 3D models from all angles

Advantages of CAM

- High level of accuracy
- Increases the speed and efficiency of the production process
- Products can be manufactured directly from CAD files
- Can operate 24 hours a day

Disadvantages of CAD

- Can be difficult to learn
- Can require large amounts of memory
- Expensive software

Disadvantages of CAM

- Expensive equipment
- Requires maintenance
- Replaces human workforce

Flexible Manufacturing Systems

Flexible manufacturing systems (FMS) consist of computer numerical control (CNC) machines that work alongside a production line. The machines are easily adaptable and can be programmed to perform different tasks depending on the product being made.

FMS is ideal for batch production and allows manufacturers to adapt quickly to consumers' changing needs by altering product designs. The layout, individual tasks and number of machines can be adjusted according to the type of product being made.

Lean Manufacturing & Just-in-Time Production

Lean manufacturing aims to minimise waste in the manufacturing process, saving money and resources and improving efficiency.

Just-in-time (JIT) is an example of lean manufacturing. Stock is closely monitored and only ordered when it is needed. The new stock then arrives 'just in time' before existing stock runs out.

Advantages of JIT

- By minimising stock levels, JIT reduces costs and limits the need for warehouse space
- Reduces the risk of losing money through stolen or damaged stock
- Stock is less likely to go out of date
- Decreases the time between ordering stock and selling the finished product to customers, helping cash flow

Disadvantages of JIT

- Lost economies of scale due to ordering of small quantities
- Lack of stock if supplier delays or ordering mistakes occur
- Increased transport costs due to more frequent deliveries
- Little room for production mistakes because of little to no stock

daydream
EDUCATION

Life Cycle Assessment

A **life cycle assessment (LCA)** is used to assess the environmental impacts of a product at every stage of its life: from obtaining the raw materials to the eventual disposal of the product.

1	Extracting, Producing and Processing Raw Materials	• How much energy is needed to extract or produce and process the raw materials? • Does extraction or production damage the environment? • Do raw materials adhere to environmental standards, (e.g. FSC wood)?
2	Manufacture	• How much energy is needed to process materials into the final product? • How much waste or pollution will manufacturing produce?
3	Distribution and Packaging	• What materials are used in packaging? • How much packaging is required? Is it unnecessarily bulky? • How much pollution will distribution cause?
4	Use	• How will using the product affect the environment? • Will the product consume a lot of energy? • Does the product produce waste or polluting substances?
5	Disposal	• How easy will it be to dispose of the product at the end of its life? • How much waste or pollution will be produced as a result of disposal?

Pollution and Global Warming

During the manufacture of many new products, fossil fuels are burned for energy production and transportation of materials. This releases greenhouse gases, such as CO_2, which many people believe cause global warming.

Warmer global temperatures are causing glaciers to melt, leading to rising sea levels and increased risk of flooding in coastal areas. Many plant and animal species are becoming extinct as their habitats are altered by rising temperatures, and severe drought is also causing famine in certain countries.

Manufacturing can also give rise to water, noise and land pollution. Factories may leak pollutants into the environment, causing harm to local wildlife, land and water supplies.

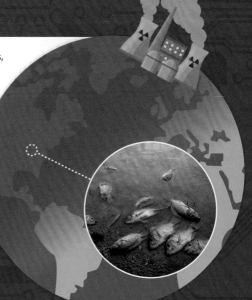

Continuous Improvement

Manufacturers are constantly looking to make small improvements to their products or processes to boost productivity and efficiency. This is known as **continuous improvement.**

Case Study: Honda's 'Green Path'

Honda's 'Green Path' is a course of action which promises to make their products more recyclable, reduce waste and carbon emissions, and conserve as many resources as possible during manufacture. Some examples of 'Green Path' in action include:

- Building two onsite wind turbines at Honda's Ohio transmission plant, which produce enough energy to power 1,000 homes for a year

- Helping to design the Auto-Max railcar, which allows more vehicles to be loaded onto a single railcar for transportation

- Implementing the Honda Environmental Leadership Program to help dealers reduce CO_2 emissions to zero

These programs have helped Honda reduce its energy use per auto by 14% over ten years.

Efficient Working

Efficient working involves making the best use of available resources to save energy and money and to minimise damage to the environment. This may be done through investment in new technology, implementing new working practices or reducing wastage during manufacture.

Some businesses employ specialist consultants in an attempt to improve efficiency.

The computer company Dell has invested in specialist technology to monitor and reduce its energy consumption at its manufacturing facilities. The technology reduces the energy used to manufacture each new product, saving money and lowering environmental impact.

When developing new products, think...

Is it made from renewable or non-renewable resources?	Does the manufacturing process cause pollution?	How much energy is used during manufacture?
Can it be disposed of easily at the end of its lifecycle?	How energy efficient will the product be?	What are the waste products?

daydream
EDUCATION

Sustainability

New and emerging technologies have led to the development of sustainable products and manufacturing processes.

Sustainability involves meeting the needs of the present without compromising the ability of future generations to meet their own needs.

When a product is manufactured, resources are consumed. Therefore, when developing a new product, designers must consider the sustainability of the resources used.

Finite Resources

Finite resources are non-renewable. They cannot be replenished as fast as they are consumed and are therefore unsustainable.

Examples: Fossil fuels (oil, gas, coal)

Non-Finite Resources

Non-finite resources are renewable. They can be replenished faster than they are consumed and are therefore sustainable.

Examples: Timber and wind power

Waste Disposal

Once a product comes to the end of its life, it must be disposed of. Historically, most waste was buried at **landfill sites**, but decaying waste can cause pollution by contaminating the local land and water supply and generating greenhouse gases.

To try and reduce the amount of waste going to landfill, people are being encouraged to recycle their waste. However, only certain materials (e.g. paper, plastic, metal) can be recycled. Food waste can be recycled for fertiliser and to generate biofuels.

Waste can also be incinerated (burned) to reduce the volume of waste going to landfill. However, this generates significant greenhouse gas emissions causing more pollution.

The 6 Rs

The 6 Rs help designers to analyse the potential environmental impact and sustainability of new products. The 6 Rs also help consumers evaluate their impact on the environment.

Rethink: Consider how the product can be made in a more sustainable way using sustainable resources and be more sustainable itself.

Reduce: We can limit the amount of resources and energy used when creating, using and disposing of products.

Refuse: We can refuse to use unsustainable and unethical resources, processes and products.

Recycle: Consider how the product can be made from recyclable materials and whether all or part of it can be recycled at the end of its life.

Repair: We can create products that are easy to repair so that their life cycle can be extended.

Reuse: Consider how the product can be used again or in other ways once it has served its function.

People

New product development is driven by new technology or changing consumer demands.

Technology Push

Sometimes a new material or technique will become available ('pushed') through research and development that enables designers to create new and exciting products.

Example: The Apple iPad

Market Pull

New product development is driven by changing consumer demands and requirements.
For example, people have recently been looking for 'greener' alternatives to plastic.

Example: Reusable coffee cups

Changing Job Roles

The rise in information technology and manufacturing automation has led to a huge reduction in manufacturing jobs and a rise in skilled jobs and service industry jobs.

Many people argue that technology often leads to redundancies and unemployment. However, others argue that technology is simply changing the nature of people's jobs. Manual work may become less common, but more skilled roles are becoming available.

Culture & Society

Different groups within society have different needs. Therefore, designers need to consider the values, cultures, customs and behaviours of different groups when developing new products.

When a product is being designed for a specific market or group, it is vital to research that market or group. Conversely, it is also important to consider the wider world, including different religions, cultures and languages, to ensure the product doesn't cause offence or have a negative impact on certain groups in society.

Fashion has a big impact on new product development. People will not purchase products that are considered 'uncool'. The Internet has enabled businesses and people (such as celebrities) to showcase new fashions and trends instantly through social media sites and blogs, resulting in trends coming and going very quickly.

People with certain **physical disabilities** or the **elderly** can find some products difficult to use. As a result, it is important to design new products that do not exclude these groups.

Products can be adapted to suit elderly people who may have poor vision or reduced mobility. For example, weighted cutlery has been specially designed to make dining easier for individuals with limited hand control.

Products can be adapted to help those with physical disabilities who may have restricted speech or mobility. For example, text-to-speech technology enables those with speech difficulties to communicate via computer.

daydream EDUCATION

Critical Evaluation & Design Decisions

When developing products, designers will analyse, test and evaluate new materials and technologies to determine their suitability for use in the products.

Planned Obsolescence

Most products are designed to have a set lifespan. Some are designed to last a long time, whereas others are designed to last for only one use. This is known as planned obsolescence.

Car
10–15 years

Mobile phone
2–3 years

Coffee pod
1 use

Single-use products do not necessarily need to be durable, but it is preferable that they are biodegradable or can be recycled. Many technology and fashion products will have intentionally short lifespans because customer demand quickly changes in response to new technologies and trends.

Some businesses use planned obsolescence to ensure a steady stream of sales. If their products last a long time, they will suffer from fewer sales. However, this is bad for the environment as it produces more waste. As such, designers must balance ethics and the environment with profit when developing new products.

Design for Maintenance

Some products are designed for maintenance. This means that when part of the product is broken or worn out, that component can be repaired or replaced without having to throw the whole product away. This is far better for the environment.

Design for disassembly is a design strategy that considers the future need to disassemble a product for repair, recycling or to prolong its life cycle.

Ethics

To keep prices low for customers, some manufacturers look for ways to cut costs during production. Sometimes this may involve behaviour that is considered unethical, such as:

- Using cheaper overseas labour
- Using cheaper materials
- Illegally disposing of waste

Some customers are willing to pay a higher price for ethically sourced, fair trade products in the knowledge that the workers can work safely and have been paid fairly.

The Environment

Designers must consider how new products will affect the environment, from their manufacture through to their disposal. Products made from renewable materials and manufactured with minimal energy consumption can help minimise damage to the environment. Using timber branded with the FSC label ensures that it has come from a sustainable source.

Ensuring new products have long lifespans, or can be recycled or reused, will also reduce the environmental impact.

FSC

Energy Generation & Storage

Sources of energy are used to generate electricity and to provide fuel for transport, heating and cooking. They can be renewable (non-finite) or non-renewable (finite).

Fossil Fuels

Fossil fuels are non-renewable natural resources formed from the remains of organisms.

The three main types of fossil fuel are coal, oil and gas. To produce electricity, fossil fuels are usually burned in power stations.

Traditionally, the UK's energy mix has consisted mainly of fossil fuels. However, declining reserves and links to climate change have led to a big shift away from fossil fuels towards renewable sources.

Coal-Fired Power Station

Advantages

- Generate large amounts of cheap energy
- Provide a reliable supply of energy

Disadvantages

- Release greenhouse gases, which cause pollution and contribute to global warming
- Will eventually run out

Renewable Energy

Renewable energy is non-finite, making it the most sustainable form of energy. However, there are several issues concerning its reliability, efficiency and initial set-up costs.

	Use	Advantages	Disadvantages
Wind	Generators in wind turbines convert the wind's kinetic energy into electricity.	Wind produces no greenhouse gases. Once turbines have been set up, energy is cheap.	Set-up costs are high. Turbines are considered unsightly and cause noise pollution.
Solar	Solar panels are used to convert the Sun's energy into electricity.	Solar energy produces no greenhouse gases. Once panels have been set up, energy is cheap.	No electricity is generated when there is no sunlight. Solar panels are expensive.
Tidal	Turbines convert kinetic energy in water currents and tides into electricity.	Tides are guaranteed, predictable and produce no greenhouse gases.	Tidal barrages are costly to build and can disrupt ecosystems.
Hydro-electric	As trapped water is released from dams, its kinetic energy turns electric turbines.	Once set up, HEP is cheap. Reservoirs provide a water supply during shortages.	Set-up costs are high. When dams are built, habitats are often destroyed.
Biomass	Organic material, such as animal waste or crops, are burned for energy or processed into biofuel.	Biomass is affordable and renewable if resources are replaced (e.g. trees are replanted).	Burning biomass releases CO_2. Also, using wood for fuel can lead to deforestation.

Nuclear Power

Nuclear power stations work in a similar way to other power stations, but heat is generated by splitting uranium atoms in nuclear reactors.

Advantages

- Very efficient – generates a lot of electricity
- Produces far less greenhouse gases than fossil fuels

Disadvantages

- Depends on a non-renewable resource (uranium)
- Produces dangerous radioactive waste products that are difficult to dispose of
- High set-up and decommissioning costs

Energy Storage Systems

Demand for energy fluctuates. Therefore, energy storage systems are needed to store electricity until it is required.

Kinetic Pumped Storage Systems

Kinetic pumped storage systems are used to manage energy supply.

When demand for energy is low (e.g. at night), excess energy produced by power stations is used to pump water from a low reservoir to a high reservoir.

When energy demand peaks (e.g. at breakfast time), water stored in the higher reservoir is released through turbines to generate extra electricity. The water is then pumped back to the higher reservoir when energy demand drops again.

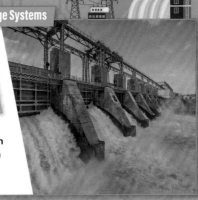

Batteries

Batteries store energy in a chemical form and convert it to electrical energy when needed.

Ordinary dry-cell batteries are non-rechargeable. As the reactants inside them are consumed in chemical reactions, the output from these batteries gradually falls. Once all the reactants have been consumed, these batteries go 'flat' and cannot supply electrical energy anymore.

Alkaline Batteries

Alkaline batteries are usually disposable and cannot be reused once flat. They leak less than other types of battery and last a long time.

Because they cannot be recharged, they are best used in devices that do not use much power (e.g. clocks and smoke detectors). Their output gradually falls over time.

Rechargeable Batteries

Rechargeable batteries can be recharged and reused so they are better for the environment than alkaline batteries.

Charging a battery reverses the chemical reaction that occurred when it was used. These batteries maintain a constant output until they go flat and are best suited to high-powered items (e.g. car batteries and mobile phones).

Batteries contain toxic chemicals that can harm the environment. Therefore, it is important that they are recycled or disposed of correctly.

15

Developments in New Materials

New materials with useful properties are constantly being developed to meet specific applications. They are developed through inventing or improving processes.

Graphene

A single layer of carbon atoms.

Properties
- transparent
- very strong and light
- excellent conductor of heat and electricity

Uses
- protective equipment and clothing
- can be mixed with paint to protect materials from corrosion
- ideal material for use in solar cells due to its transparency and conductive properties

Metal Foams

Metals are injected with air whilst in a liquid state.

Properties
- lightweight
- strong under compression, so absorb energy well
- low thermal conductivity

Uses
- prosthetics (artificial body parts)
- ideal for use in soundproofing and crash protection in vehicles due to its ability to absorb energy

Titanium

A metal that has historically been difficult to extract, refine and process.

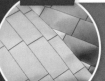

Properties
- high strength-to-weight ratio
- corrosion-resistant
- can withstand extreme temperatures
- expensive

Uses
- prosthetics (artificial body parts)
- ideal for use in aircraft and spacecraft, due to its resistance to corrosion and high strength-to-weight ratio
- often alloyed with other metals

Modern materials are also developed through altering existing materials.

Coated Metals

Properties of metals can be improved by adding a coating of another material, often to increase strength and resistance to corrosion. Examples include, nickel-plated steel, polymer-coated aluminium and galvanised steel (applying a protective zinc coating).

Liquid Crystal Displays (LCDs)

LCDs are flat panel displays that use liquid crystals to control light emission and create an image. When voltage is applied to liquid crystals, they change shape and allow different levels of light to pass through, thereby creating an image.

Nanomaterials

Nanomaterials contain particles less than 100 nanometres in size and have different properties to larger particles of the same material. They have a large surface-area-to-volume ratio, which can improve properties such as strength, conductivity and reactivity.

daydream EDUCATION

Smart Materials

The properties of smart materials change in response to external stimuli, such as stress, temperature, moisture or pH.

Shape Memory Alloys (SMAs)
SMAs are metal alloys with memory properties. They can return to their original shape after being deformed through heating or applying an electrical current. Nitinol®, an alloy of nickel and titanium, is an SMA.

Thermochromic materials change colour in response to changes in temperature. In thermochromic liquid crystals, the crystals re-orientate as the temperature changes, causing a change in colour.
Thermochromic Pigments

Photochromic Pigments
Photochromic materials change colour in response to changes in light levels. They can be used in glasses, so the lenses get lighter or darker, depending on light levels.

Composite Materials

Composite materials are made from two or more materials, often ones with contrasting properties. Combining the properties of two different materials can lead to the development of new and improved materials. Concrete is one of the most common composite materials.

Glass reinforced plastic (GRP) combines glass fibres with a thermosetting plastic to create a lightweight, strong and resistant material that is used in boat hulls and car bodies.

Carbon reinforced plastic (CRP) combines carbon fibres with a thermosetting plastic. It is more rigid, stronger and lighter than GRP, but it is also more expensive and brittle.

Technical Textiles

Some textiles are manufactured for functionality rather than aesthetics.

Kevlar® is a strong synthetic textile with a high tensile strength-to-weight ratio. It is often used in protective armour.

Conductive textiles conduct electricity. Metal fibres are either spun into the fabric or metal-based powders are impregnated into the fabric.

Fire-resistant fabrics, such as Nomex® have flame resistance built into their chemical structures to protect the wearer.

Microfibres are made of extremely fine synthetic fibres. They are breathable and durable, so are often used in sports clothing. They can also be **microencapsulated** to incorporate tiny capsules that are capable of holding substances such as scents, therapeutic oils and insecticides. Over time, the capsules rupture, releasing the contents.

17

Electronic Systems

A system is made up of several parts that work together as a whole to carry out a function. All electronic systems require an **input**, a **process** and an **output**.

Input		Process		Output
Key on keyboard pressed	→	CPU processed input data into output data	→	Monitor displays the processed data

Systems diagrams clearly show the input, process and output stages of a system. The more complex the system, the more blocks there are in the diagram.

Circuits

An electrical circuit is a closed circuit that contains a sequence of components that are connected by wires to a source of power.

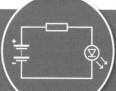

- In electronic systems, circuit diagrams are used to show how a circuit works.
- Symbols are used to represent electrical components.
- Voltage from the power cell pushes the current around the circuit.
- In a circuit, the direction of the electrical current is from positive to negative.

A printed circuit board (PCB) supports and connects electronic components.

- PCBs are non-conductive boards that contain copper tracks that link holes where electrical components can be inserted.
- They are designed specifically for each circuit.
- Components are attached directly onto the surface of a PCB. This is known as surface mounting.

daydream
EDUCATION

Some input devices (e.g. switches) are manually triggered, whereas others (e.g. burglar alarms) are triggered by movement or environmental changes (e.g. light, temperature or pressure). Input devices trigger the system, sending an electrical signal to be processed.

Switches

- Switches are used to complete or disconnect a circuit.
- A switch can be turned on (closed) to let current flow or turned off (open) to stop current flow.
- Switches come in many forms, including toggles, slides, pushes and microswitches.

Light-Dependent Resistors (LDRs)

- LDRs detect changes in light levels.
- Resistance increases in the dark (limiting the current) and decreases in the light (increasing the current).
- LDRs are often used in items such as street lights that come on automatically when it gets dark.

Thermistors

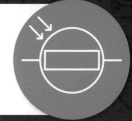

- Thermistors are resistors that detect changes in temperature.
- Resistance decreases as temperature increases (increasing the current) and increases as temperature decreases (limiting the current).
- They are often used in air conditioning systems that turn on when the temperature rises.

Pressure Sensors

- Pressure sensors detect changes in pressure.
- Depending on the sensor's function, resistance either increases or decreases to allow more or less current to flow through.
- Sensors are often used in car tyres to notify drivers when air pressure drops below a certain level.

Process Devices

Process devices process the electronic signals received from an input to determine an output action.

Most processes in electronic systems are carried out by **integrated circuits (ICs)** that can perform multiple tasks, thus reducing the number of components needed in a circuit.

Microcontrollers

A **microcontroller** is a type of IC that is programmed to perform specific tasks in a wide variety of electronic devices. It contains memory, programmable input/output peripherals and a processor all on one chip – it is essentially a tiny computer.

Microcontrollers are adaptable and can be programmed to perform different tasks. The program is then stored in the microcontroller's memory.

Programs are written in a special programming language. Alternatively, a flowchart can be used and then translated by special software into coded commands for the microcontroller. Common programming languages include embedded C, Python, BASIC and Scratch.

Microcontrollers are often used as **timers** and **counters** in embedded systems to measure elapsed time or to count or time external events.

Start → Input → Process → Decision → No / Yes → Output → End

Timers

Timers are often used to add a time delay. They do this by creating a pulse of voltage after a certain period of time to trigger an output. An example includes a microwave timer.

Counters

Counters count the number of pulses of voltage created by an input device and display this as an output. An example includes a pedometer, which counts each step a person takes.

Decision-Making

Circuits can be programmed to make decisions based on situations.
Logic gates make decisions in microcontrollers based on whether an input is on (1) or off (0).

NOT gates

Take one input and output the opposite value.

Example: If its emergency button is pressed (1), a treadmill will stop (0).

AND gates

Take at least two inputs and identify if all values are 1. If all inputs are 1, it outputs 1; otherwise, 0 is the output.

Example: If a burglar alarm is turned on (1) and the sensor detects movement (1), the alarm will sound (1).

OR gates

Take at least two inputs and identify if any of the values are 1. If at least one input is 1, it outputs 1; otherwise, 0 is the output.

Example: If the increase volume button is pressed on the TV (1) or the remote control (1), the volume will get louder.

daydream EDUCATION

Output Devices

Output devices transfer electrical energy into a response depending on the device's function.

Buzzers

- Buzzers use electrical energy to create sound energy.
- Most use a piezo transducer, which converts electrical current into mechanical movement, to create sound.

Example: car alarm

Speakers

- Speakers use electrical energy to create sound energy.

Example: speakers on a mobile phone

Lamps

- Lamps convert electrical energy into light energy.

Example: house lights

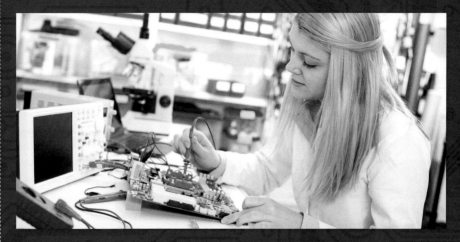

daydream EDUCATION

Mechanisms

Mechanical devices change an input force and movement into a desired output force and movement. They can change the magnitude and direction of force.

Input

Force and movement are input into a mechanism

Mechanism

The mechanism converts or transmits the input force and movement into an output force and movement.

Output

Force and movement are output to satisfy a need

Mechanisms can be used to make a force bigger or smaller.

Movement

Mechanical devices can be used to produce different types of movement.

Linear	Reciprocating	Rotary	Oscillating
Movement in a straight line in one direction	Movement in a straight line in two directions	Rotational movement on or around an axis	Movement back and forth along a curved path

Simple Mechanisms

Inclined plane

Screw

Wheel & axle

Wedge

Lever

Pulley

Mechanical advantage (MA) is a measure of the force amplification achieved by using a mechanism.

The mechanical advantage measures the ratio of the input force (effort) to the output force (load).

$$MA = \frac{Load}{Effort}$$

daydream
EDUCATION

Gears

Gears are toothed wheels attached to shafts. They are used to transmit power and rotational motion around mechanical systems.

Gear Trains

Gear trains consist of two or more interlocking gears that transmit **torque** (the turning force that causes rotation) and rotary motion.

- The teeth on the gears interlock to prevent slipping.
- The input gear is the driver gear.
- The output gear is the **driven gear**.
- If the driver gear rotates clockwise, the **driven gear** rotates **anticlockwise** and **vice versa**.

In this example, the driver gear is rotating clockwise. Therefore, the driven gear is rotating anticlockwise.

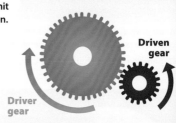

Driven gear

Driver gear

Changing Direction

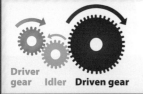

Driver gear   Idler   Driven gear

The direction of rotation of the driven gear can be changed by adding an **idler gear**. The idler gear changes the direction of rotation so that both the driver gear and driven gear are moving in the same direction.

The size of the idler gear does not matter: it transfers the movement, without altering the speed of the gears.

Changing Speed

Gears can be used to make the output speed faster or slower than the input speed by using different-sized gears.

Creating a Faster Output Speed

To make the output speed faster, the input gear must be larger than the output gear.

Driver gear (40 teeth)   Driven gear (20 teeth)

Creating a Slower Output Speed

To make the output speed slower, the input gear must be smaller than the output gear.

Driver gear (10 teeth)   Driven gear (30 teeth)

Calculating Gear Ratios

The larger gear always equals 1. The smaller gear is calculated by dividing the number of teeth on the larger gear by the number of teeth on the smaller gear.

In the example above:

Driver	Gear Ratio	Driven
= 1	1 : 2	= 40 ÷ 20 = 2

1 turn of the driver gear = 2 turns of the driven gear

In the example above:

Driver	Gear Ratio	Driven
= 30 ÷ 10 = 3	3 : 1	= 1

3 turns of the driver gear = 1 turn of the driven gear

23

Cams & Followers

Cam mechanisms are used to convert rotary motion into reciprocal motion. Mechanisms consist of a cam and a follower.

A **cam** is a specially shaped piece of material attached to a rotating shaft.

A rod known as a **follower** rests on the **cam** and rises and falls as the cam rotates, creating a reciprocating motion.

Depending on the shape of the cam, the follower will either rise, fall or dwell (remain stationary).

Follower

Cam

Slide

Wheel follower

Crank

A cam mechanism will often also include:

- A **slide** to prevent the follower from slipping
- A **crank** (handle) to manually rotate the camshaft
- A **wheel follower** to reduce friction between the cam and follower

Types of Cam

Cams come in a variety of shapes and sizes. Common examples include:

Eccentric (Circular)

The pivot (rotating shaft) is positioned off-centre, causing the follower to steadily rise and fall.

Pear-Shaped

The follower dwells (remains stationary) for half a turn. It then rises as the point approaches for a quarter of a turn before falling for the last quarter rotation.

Snail

The follower gradually rises and then suddenly drops. It can only rotate in one direction.

Heart-Shaped (Constant Velocity)

The follower rises and falls with no dwell period. It is said to have constant velocity.

daydream EDUCATION

Pulleys & Belts

Pulleys

A simple fixed pulley mechanism is made up of a rimmed wheel and cable, which sits inside the rimmed wheel.

It provides no mechanical advantage, but it can make items easier to lift by changing the direction of force.

100-kg lifting force

100 kg

Using two or more pulleys together (in a **block and tackle** system) can reduce the magnitude of force required to lift a load.

The example shown will halve the required input force to lift the load.

50-kg lifting force

100 kg

Belt & Pulley Systems

In a belt and pulley system, two or more pulleys are connected by a belt to transfer rotary motion and force from the driver pulley, to the driven pulley. These systems are used in car engines and washing machines. Belts need to remain taut, so they are often made of rubber to reduce slippage.

Belts can be crossed to change the direction of the output movement.

Driver pulley · Driven pulley · Belt · Driver pulley · Driven pulley

Calculating the Velocity Ratio

Using different-sized wheels changes the speed and force of rotation (torque).

When the driver pulley is larger than the driven pulley, the driven pulley will rotate faster, but the torque will be less.

When the driver pulley is smaller than the driven pulley, the driven pulley will rotate slower, but the torque will be greater.

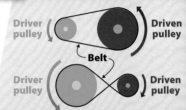

The velocity ratio between the two pulleys can be calculated using the following formula:

$$\text{Velocity ratio} = \frac{\text{Diameter of driven pulley}}{\text{Diameter of driver pulley}}$$

Driver pulley — 5 cm — 15 cm — **Driven pulley**

$$\text{Velocity ratio} = \frac{15}{5} = \frac{3}{1} = 3:1$$

The velocity ratio shows that the driver pulley will rotate three times slower than the driven pulley. However, the torque of the driven pulley will be greater.

Levers & Linkages

A lever is a mechanical device used to transmit and transform the effects of forces. The input force (effort) + motion is transmitted through the lever to move the load.

There are three parts to a lever:

Effort
1
The input force exerted on the lever

Fulcrum/Pivot
2
The point around which the lever acts

Load
3
The force of the object that needs to be moved

There are three classes of levers:

First Order Levers

In a first order lever, the fulcrum is positioned between the load and the effort. The input effort required to lift the load can be reduced by moving the fulcrum closer to the load.

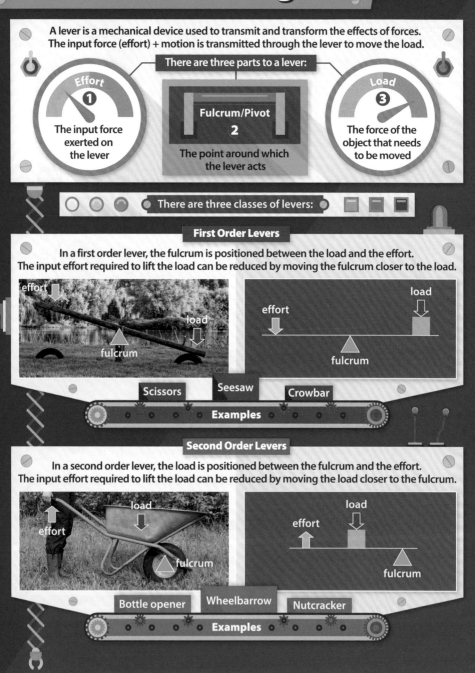

effort — load — fulcrum

effort — load — fulcrum

Examples
Scissors   Seesaw   Crowbar

Second Order Levers

In a second order lever, the load is positioned between the fulcrum and the effort. The input effort required to lift the load can be reduced by moving the load closer to the fulcrum.

load — effort — fulcrum

load — effort — fulcrum

Examples
Bottle opener   Wheelbarrow   Nutcracker

daydream EDUCATION

Third Order Levers

In a third order lever, the effort is positioned between the fulcrum and the load. Third order levers do not have the mechanical advantage of first order and second order levers. The effort is closer to the fulcrum than the load. As a result, the input effort is greater than the output force.

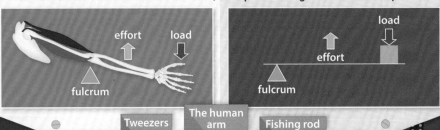

Examples

Tweezers — The human arm — Fishing rod

Linkages

Levers can be joined together to make linkages.
Linkages change an input motion + force into an output motion + force.
They often transmit force and motion at a distance from the initial input.

Push/Pull Linkages

A push/pull or parallel motion linkage creates an identical parallel motion at the output.

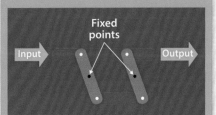

Bell Crank Linkages

A bell crank linkage changes the direction of motion through 90 degrees.

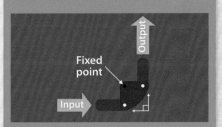

Changing Magnitude of Force

In the reverse linkage below, the fixed point (pivot) is an equal distance from the input and output levers, so the output force is equal to the input force.

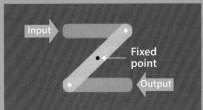

To make the output force greater than the input force, move the fixed point closer to the output.

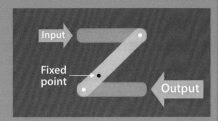

Material Properties

During the design process, it is important to know the physical and working properties of potential materials.

Physical Properties

Physical properties relate to the actual material.

Absorbency — The ability of a material to take in or soak up something (usually a liquid, but sometimes heat and light). Papers, boards and natural fibres are generally good absorbers of liquids.

Density — A material's mass per unit volume (how compact it is). It is commonly measured in g/cm^3 or kg/cm^3. Metals are usually dense.

Fusibility — The ability of a material to be converted into a molten or liquid state through heating. Materials that convert into their molten state at a low melting point, such as solder, have a high fusibility. Solder is used to fuse together other metals because it melts before the metals being joined melt.

Electrical Conductivity — The ability of a material to conduct electricity. Metals are generally good electrical conductors, and plastics tend to be poor electrical conductors (insulators). As a result, electrical wiring is often made from copper and encased in a flexible plastic.

Thermal Conductivity — The ability of a material to conduct heat. Metals are generally good thermal conductors, and plastics tend to be poor thermal conductors (insulators). As a result, frying pans are often made from aluminium with plastic handles.

Working Properties

Working properties relate to how a material responds to external forces and/or conditions.

Strength — The ability of a material to withstand force without breaking. Examples of forces include pressure, tension, compression, shear and torsion. Materials may be strong in one force but weak in another (e.g. concrete is strong in compression but weak in tension).

Hardness — The ability of a material to resist wear, abrasion, scratching or denting. Diamond is the hardest naturally occurring substance found on Earth.

Toughness — The ability of a material to absorb energy without fracturing

Malleability — The ability of a material to be bent and shaped without breaking

Ductility — The ability of a material to be stretched or pulled into a strand without breaking

Elasticity — The ability of a material to return to its original shape after being stretched, bent or compressed

Papers & Boards

Papers and boards are made from natural fibres (cellulose) from wood and recycled waste paper. Papers and boards have different properties and functions.

Paper and board are classified based on their weight in grams per square metre (**gsm**).

Anything that weighs under 200 gsm is generally considered paper.

200 gsm

Anything that weighs over 200 gsm is generally considered board.

Types of Paper

Name	Physical Properties	Uses
Bleed-proof paper	A smooth, thick paper that prevents ink from seeping and bleeding	Quality presentational drawings
Cartridge paper	Creamy white paper, usually with a lightly textured surface	Drawings (pencil, charcoal, pastel) and paintings
Grid paper	White paper with a printed grid of isometric lines or squares	Scale drawings, quick sketches and model-making
Layout paper	Thin, relatively transparent paper with a smooth surface	General design work and sometimes tracing
Tracing paper	Thin, transparent paper with a smooth surface	Copying and tracing designs

Types of Board

Name	Physical Properties	Uses
Corrugated card	Two or more layers of card with a fluted layer in between to add strength	Packaging and boxes to protect items from damage
Duplex board	Cheaper than white card, usually has one smooth white side (often printed)	Food packaging that requires printing on one side
Foil-lined board	Card lined with aluminium foil on one side to provide insulation	Takeaway food packaging
Foam core board	Two thin layers of card with a foam inner core in between	Model-making and mounting pictures
Inkjet card	Smooth, treated card for a high-quality, bleed-proof finish	High-quality photographs
Solid white board	Strong, high-quality bleached card that is perfect for printing	High-quality packaging, printing and book covers

daydream
EDUCATION

29

Natural Timbers

Wood is an organic material that is the main substance in the trunk and branches of a tree. Wood prepared for use in building and carpentry is known as *timber*.

Hardwoods

Most hardwoods come from broad-leaved, deciduous trees (trees that shed their leaves annually). They are generally slow growing and are therefore usually more scarce and expensive than softwoods.

Beech
- hard, tough, strong & finishes well
- warps easily
- close, straight grain
- expensive
- pinkish-brown

Uses
- flooring
- furniture
- tool handles

Oak
- very strong, heavy, durable & hard
- grain varies but is generally open
- over 400 species
- light brown

Uses
- flooring
- furniture
- barrels

Mahogany
- hard, strong, easy to work & resistant to rot
- fine, straight grain
- some species are protected
- reddish-brown

Uses
- flooring
- fine furniture
- instruments

Balsa
- very light & soft, but has great strength-to-weight ratio
- straight grain with distinct velvety feel
- pale cream to white

Uses
- surfboards
- construction & aircraft models

Other hardwoods include ash, birch, maple and willow.

Softwoods come from coniferous trees that have long needle-like leaves and are generally found in cold climates. They are quick growing and can therefore be replaced quicker than hardwoods.

Softwoods

Cedar
- contains a chemical that makes it durable & resistant to weather
- short, notable grain
- light cream to reddish-brown

Uses
- outdoor furniture
- cupboards
- fencing

Scots Pine
- easy to work with, reasonably strong & lightweight
- straight grain with lots of knots
- pale to reddish-brown

Uses
- furniture
- construction
- door frames

Larch
- tough & strong, but easy to work
- resistant to rot, but prone to splitting
- yellow to reddish-brown

Uses
- decking
- cladding
- fencing

Spruce
- good strength-to-weight ratio
- can contain small knots
- creamy white to pinkish-brown

Uses
- construction
- stringed musical instruments

Other softwoods include Douglas fir, yew and western hemlock.

Remember: Not all hardwoods are hard, and not all softwoods are soft.

daydream EDUCATION

Manufactured Boards

Manufactured boards are made from fibres, chips, blocks or sheets of wood bonded together with adhesives.

Medium-Density Fibreboard (MDF)

Woodchips are broken down into a pulp (small fibres), mixed with glue and compressed.

MDF

- Has a smooth surface, which makes it easy to paint and finish (often with a higher-quality veneer)
- Denser than other manufactured boards
- Produces a lot of hazardous dust (a mask must be worn when working with it).
- Used in flat-pack furniture, kitchen units and interior panelling; comes in moisture-and-fire-resistant varieties

Plywood

Alternate layers of wood (veneers) are glued together at 90 degrees to each other.

Plywood

- Very strong in all directions; often stronger than solid wood
- Outside layers are finished with a higher-quality veneer
- Must always include an odd number of layers and the grain always runs in the same direction on the outside layers
- Used in construction (roofing and cladding) and furniture
- Comes in water-resistant marine grades for use in boats

Chipboard

Small chips of wood are compressed and glued together.

Chipboard

- Has a rough surface and texture so is often covered with veneers to improve its appearance
- Low-cost but not as strong or durable as other manufactured timber, such as MDF
- Easily damaged by moisture but comes in water-resistant varieties
- Used for low-cost furniture, kitchen worktops and shelving

Metals & Alloys

Metals are elements that are usually found in rocks called ores. Most metals have to be industrially extracted from the earth through mining.

Metals that contain only a single metal are known as pure metals. Gold, silver, platinum and copper are the only metals found in nature in their pure form.

Metals are usually good conductors of heat and electricity and have a high density and lustre. Most can be recycled.

Ferrous Metals

Ferrous metals contain iron. Almost all ferrous metals are magnetic and, unless treated, rust. Ferrous metals become harder and stronger, but less malleable, as more carbon is added.

Low-Carbon Steel
0.01–0.30% carbon

- Malleable and reasonably tough
- Cannot be hardened and tempered
- Inexpensive but rusts easily

Uses: car bodies, nails and screws

High-Carbon (Tool) Steel
0.6–1.5% carbon

- Very hard but brittle
- Difficult to cut and work
- Can be hardened and tempered
- Prone to rust

Uses: drill bits, tools and springs

Cast Iron
2–4% carbon

- Hard but brittle so cannot be bent or forged
- Resistant to deformation, wear and rust
- Strong under compression but not under tension

Uses: manhole covers and car brake discs

daydream EDUCATION

Non-Ferrous Metals

Non-ferrous metals do not contain iron. They are not magnetic. Compared to ferrous metals, they are generally more resistant to corrosion and more expensive.

Aluminium

- Durable, lightweight and resistant to corrosion
- A good conductor of heat and electricity

Uses: drinks cans, aircrafts and foil

Copper

- Relatively soft, malleable and ductile
- A great conductor of heat and electricity

Uses: electrical wiring, central heating pipes

Tin

- Soft, malleable and ductile
- High resistance to corrosion
- Has a low melting point

Uses: tin can coating and solder

Zinc

- Weak but malleable once heated
- High resistance to corrosion
- Has a low melting point

Uses: galvanising (coating steel)

Alloys

Metals are alloyed (mixed with other metals or elements) to improve their physical properties.

Brass
copper and zinc

Stainless Steel
iron, carbon and a minimum of 10.5% chromium

High-Speed Steel
various elements such as carbon, tungsten and chromium

- Combined to increase hardness
- A good conductor of electricity
- Resistant to corrosion

Uses: musical instruments, keys and taps

- Tough, hard, strong and difficult to cut
- High resistance to corrosion if chromium and nickel are added

Uses: cutlery, surgical equipment and sinks

- Strong and remains hard even when heated
- Can cut at high speeds and high temperatures

Uses: cutting tools (e.g. mill cutters), power saw blades and drill bits

Polymers

Polymers, such as plastics, are man-made materials that are used in a wide range of products.

Thermosetting Polymers

Thermosetting polymers undergo a chemical change when formed that makes them permanently rigid and resistant to heat and fire. They cannot be re-formed and are not recyclable.

Epoxy Resin (ER)

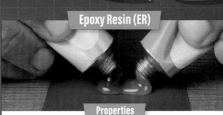

Properties

Hard, brittle and durable; a good electrical insulator

Uses

Adhesives, castings and circuit boards

Melamine Formaldehyde (MF)

Properties

Hard, strong and highly resistant to heat, light, chemicals, fire and wear

Uses

Tableware and kitchen worktops

Phenol Formaldehyde (PF)

Properties

A good electrical insulator; hard and highly resistant to heat and chemicals

Uses

Electrical fittings and saucepan handles

Polyester Resin (PR)

Properties

Hard and brittle but becomes tough when mixed with glass strands to create glass-reinforced plastic (GRP)

Uses

Boat hulls, kayaks and car panels

Urea Formaldehyde (UF)

Properties

Hard, brittle and heat resistant; a good electrical insulator

Uses

Electrical fittings and door handles

daydream
EDUCATION

Thermoforming Polymers

Thermoforming polymers contain few cross-linkage molecules, so they are not very resistant to heat. They can easily be melted, moulded and often re-formed. They are also recyclable.

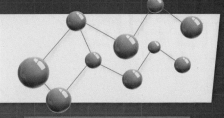

Acrylic (PMMA)

Properties

Hard, shiny and resistant to weathering but scratches easily

Uses

Baths and signage; as a glass substitute

High-Impact Polystyrene (HIPS)

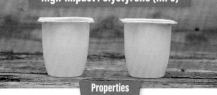

Properties

Hard, rigid, lightweight and suitable for vacuum forming

Uses

Food pots and casings

High-Density Polyethylene (HDPE)

Properties

Tough, strong and flexible with a good chemical resistance

Uses

Buckets, bins and drinks bottles

Polypropylene (PP)

Properties

Tough, lightweight and flexible with a strong chemical resistance

Uses

Stationery, food packaging and rope

Polyvinyl Chloride (PVC)

Properties

Can be rigid or flexible; cheap and durable (resistant to weathering)

Uses

Guttering, raincoats and window sills

Polyethylene Terephthalate (PET)

Properties

Tough, strong, lightweight and durable

Uses

Drinks bottles and food packaging

Textiles

Textiles are materials made from natural or synthetic fibres. Their properties vary depending on their compositional material and how they are formed.

Natural Fibres

Natural fibres come from **biological** sources (plants and animals). They are renewable and biodegradable.

Name	Image	Properties	Uses
Cotton Sourced from the cotton plant		Strong, highly absorbent and cool to wear in hot weather. It is also easy to dye and wash. However, it creases easily, can shrink and is flammable.	Clothing, upholstery and towels.
Wool Sourced from animal fleece (mainly sheep)		Soft, warm and absorbent. It is also crease-resistant and has low flammability. However, it can shrink and takes a long time to dry.	Jumpers, rugs, blankets, coats, carpets
Silk Sourced from silkworm cocoons		Lightweight, smooth and soft. It has a lustre due to its fibre's triangular structure. However, it is expensive, weak when wet and creases easily.	Dresses, ties, soft furnishings and upholstery.

Synthetic Fibres

Synthetic fibres are polymers **manufactured from chemical sources or fossil fuels**. Therefore, most synthetic fibres are not sustainable or biodegradable.

Name	Image	Properties	Uses
Polyester		Strong and durable with low flammability. It is also non-absorbent and resistant to creases and biological damage. However, it is not very warm.	Sportswear, raincoats, bedsheets, rope, bedding
Polyamide (nylon)		Lightweight but strong and hard-wearing. It is also crease-resistant, warm and non-absorbent. However, it is easily damaged by sunlight.	Ropes, sportswear, tights, swimwear
Elastane (Lycra®)		Smooth, strong and very stretchy (elastic). It keeps its shape well and is crease resistant. However, it is highly flammable.	Sportswear, swimwear, leggings, underwear

daydream
EDUCATION

Blended and Mixed Fibres

Blended fabrics are made by spinning two or more types of fibre together to produce a yarn (thread). Fabrics are blended to combine different fibres with desirable properties.

Polycotton (cotton and polyester) is more durable, cheaper and stronger than cotton alone and is less likely to crease or shrink. However, it is not as breathable and is highly flammable.

Woven Fabrics

Woven fabrics are made by interlacing two sets of yarn at right (90°) angles to each other. The **weft** runs along the **width** of the fabric, and the **warp** runs along the **length** of the fabric.

Woven fabrics tend to be very strong, particularly along the **straight grain** (warp) of the fabric. The edge of a woven fabric is known as a **selvedge**, and it will not fray unless cut.

The plain weave is the most basic and cheapest weave to produce. It is made by passing the weft yarn over and under warp yarns. It is strong, hard-wearing and holds its shape well. Its pattern is identical on both sides of the fabric.

Non-Woven Fabrics

Non-woven fabrics are made directly from fibres that have not been spun into yarns.

Bonded Fabric

Bonded fabric is made from webs of fibres that are bonded together with glue, heat, stitches or needle-punching. Fabrics do not fray but are weak.

Uses: disposable cloths, tea bags, clothing

Felted Fabric

Felt is made from matting wool fibres together by using moisture, heat and pressure. It is inelastic and pulls apart easily.

Uses: jewellery, hats, crafts, carpet underlay

Knitted Fabrics

Knitted fabrics are made by **interlocking** (rather than interlacing) loops of yarn together.

Weft Knitting

Weft-knit fabric is made by hand or machine using a yarn that forms interlocking loops across the width of the fabric.

It is stretchy and warm. However, it can lose its shape and unravel easily.

Warp Knitting

Warp-knit fabric is made by machine using yarn that forms vertical interlocking loops.

It is less stretchy than weft-knitted fabric, but it retains its shape better and is less likely to unravel.

Selecting Materials

Designers should consider various factors when choosing materials or components for a product.

Functionality

When selecting a material for a given application, designers must ensure the material is fit for purpose. To do this, they must consider how the product will be used and which properties the material will need to perform its intended function.

As well as considering the function of the product, designers must also consider the ease of working with the materials.

Aesthetics

Most people want products that look good. Therefore, when selecting materials and components, designers must consider aesthetic factors such as colour, texture and surface finish.

Example

Dan is designing a bedside cabinet as part of a luxury bedroom furniture range. As well as considering the functional capabilities of potential materials, he must consider:

- **Colour:** Does the colour match the other items in the range?
- **Texture:** Does the texture feel appealing?
- **Surface finish:** Will the wood be waxed, varnished or painted?
- Does it match the other items in the range?

Environmental Factors

It is important to consider the sustainability of potential materials and how their extraction, use and disposal will affect the environment.

- How easy is it to extract the materials?
- Are the materials renewable and sustainable?
- Are the materials locally sourced or easy to transport?
- Can the materials be reused?
- Are the materials biodegradable or recyclable?

Availability

Some materials are easier to source than others, so designers must consider the availability of materials. Many materials are only available in stock sizes. This helps maximise efficiency and productivity, reducing cost. Materials that are scarce, difficult to transport or are a long distance away are likely to be more expensive.

Cost

Affordable

Designers must consider raw material, manufacturing, packaging and shipping costs, as well as the selling price. The cost of materials and manufacture should not exceed the final price of the product.

Selected materials should match the value of the overall product. Using expensive materials in a budget product will not be financially viable. Also, people will not pay high-end prices for budget materials.

Luxury

Bulk-buying enables manufacturers to negotiate a discount from suppliers. In turn, they can then produce products at a lower cost, enabling them to charge customers a lower price or make a bigger profit.

Cultural Factors

Culture encompasses the ideas, customs and social behaviour of a group in society. In a multicultural society, how one group receives a product may differ entirely from how another group does. Designers must therefore remain culturally sensitive when designing products.

Example: The Bank of England received thousands of complaints from the vegan community after releasing new banknotes that contain traces of animal fat.

Social and Ethical Factors

Designers have a responsibility to consider a product's impact on society. This is true even if it means paying more money for ethically sourced materials that are environmentally sustainable and that support the well-being of workers.

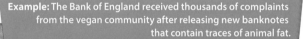

Unethical products include those that damage the environment or exploit people in their production.

For example, the increased production of cheap palm oil has resulted in large areas of rainforest being destroyed to make way for palm plantations. This has caused loss of animal habitats and significant amounts of pollution due to extraction. Large scale deforestation also contributes to the greenhouse effect and climate change.

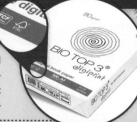

Products that carry the FSC logo have been approved by the Forest Stewardship Council.

This means that the wood or paper used in the product has come from a sustainable source.

Forces & Stresses

Forces apply stress to objects, causing them to break or change shape. Different materials can withstand different forces.

Force is measured in newtons (N), and **stress** (the force acting on a unit area) is measured in newtons per square metre (N/m^2). Strong materials are able to withstand large forces without breaking. There are different types of forces.

Tension

Tension is a stretching or pulling force.

Compression

Compression is a squashing or pushing force.

Bending

Bending is a combination of tension and compression forces. It exerts tension on one side of an object and compression on the other.

Shear

Shear is a cutting force. The opposing forces are not directly opposite each other.

Torsion

Torsion is a twisting force that attempts to rotate two ends of a material in opposite directions.

daydream EDUCATION

Enhancing Materials

Materials and objects can be manipulated to resist and work with forces and stresses. This may involve them being reinforced, stiffened or made more flexible.

Lamination

Lamination involves adding layers to a material to form a composite. The addition of layers increases the material's strength, rigidity and sometimes flexibility.

Paper can be laminated in a plastic pouch to create a stronger, more durable and water-resistant sheet.

In plywood, layers of wood are compressed and glued at 90° to each other to increase strength.

It is also possible to laminate fabric to increase durability and strength.

Interfacing

Interfacing is often used in textiles to add strength to materials.

Extra layers of fabric are ironed (fusible interfacing) or sewn (sew-in interfacing) onto the unseen side of garments to maintain shape and add strength and rigidity. It is often used in shirt collars and cuffs and in baseball caps to add rigidity.

Webbing

Webbing is woven into strips to give it high tensile strength. It is often used in items that are subjected to a lot of tension, such as seatbelts and strapping used to secure heavy equipment.

Often made from synthetic fibres, webbing is lightweight and flexible.

Bending

Bending materials to form curves, arches and tubes can stiffen and strengthen them significantly.

Corrugated card incorporates a fluted layer between two outside sheets, which makes it a lot stronger and rigid. Chair and table legs are usually curved and shaped in a specific way for added strength.

Folding

Folding creates a crease between two sides of a bend. This adds strength and flexibility enabling materials to bend more easily.

A piece of paper placed over a gap (like a bridge) will not withstand a lot of added weight. However, when paper is folded into a concertina shape it can hold more weight.

Ecological & Social Issues

When designing new products, designers must consider the environmental impact of sourcing, transporting and manufacturing potential materials.

Deforestation

Deforestation is the clearing of rainforests and wooded areas. Trees are felled to make room for grazing animals, or to harvest pulp and wood for paper and timber, resulting in the loss of animal habitats.

Deforestation also contributes to climate change. Trees remove CO_2 from the atmosphere, so fewer trees means increased CO_2 levels in the atmosphere contributing to the greenhouse effect and rising global temperatures.

Mining

Coal, metals and minerals are extracted from the ground through mining, which causes huge amounts of damage to the environment. Large areas of land must be cleared to make room for mines, causing various forms of pollution and worsening the impact of deforestation.

Mining also requires lots of energy. To provide this energy, large amounts of fossil fuels are burned, releasing CO_2 into the atmosphere and depleting reserves of finite, non-renewable resources.

Drilling

Oil and gas are finite, unsustainable resources that are extracted from land or sea through drilling. They are fossil fuels that are also used to produce plastic.

Drilling can cause various forms of land and sea pollution. Waste products pollute the environment and oil spills can have disastrous effects on marine habitats, killing marine plants and animals.

Farming

Biofuels and plants used to make new materials are grown on farms.

Animal (livestock) farming requires large areas of land for grazing, resulting in the destruction of natural habitats, including forests, and reduced biodiversity. Chemical pesticides and fertilisers used to increase crop yields can leak into the local water and soil, polluting habitats and killing wildlife.

daydream
EDUCATION

Carbon Footprint

The amount of carbon dioxide released by a product during its life cycle is known as its carbon footprint. Consider the bed opposite.

- How much carbon is produced during extraction, processing and manufacture?
- How many miles have the materials travelled?
- Does the product cause any pollution or use any energy during its life?
- How much energy is required to dispose of or recycle the materials at the end of its life?

Steel from China

Wood from Brazil

Polyester from India

Although the bed does not cause any pollution during its use, the amount of carbon produced during extraction, processing, manufacture and transport is likely to be extremely high.

Safe Working Conditions

In the UK, laws such as the Health and Safety at Work Act 1974 protect the health, rights and safety of workers, whilst other laws exist to address issues such as discrimination, working hours and paid leave. Employers also must provide safety equipment and training.

Unfortunately, not all countries provide the same protections for workers. As a result, workers are often exploited and forced to work long hours for a very low wage and in unsafe conditions.

Businesses have an ethical responsibility to ensure the rights of workers across their supply chain, from extraction through to distribution.

Reducing Pollution

The manufacture of products can cause various forms of pollution.

Ocean Pollution

Almost 8 million tons of plastic per year ends up in the world's oceans, damaging habitats and killing marine wildlife. Oil spills and chemicals from industrial waste, such as mercury, also contribute greatly to water pollution.

To reduce ocean pollution, there needs to be a significant reduction in the use of plastic and an increase in recycling rates.

Atmospheric Pollution

The burning of fossil fuels releases greenhouse gases such as CO_2 and SO_2 into the atmosphere, resulting in air pollution. Air pollution is particularly problematic in industrial areas and can cause respiratory health problems.

To reduce air pollution, there needs to be a shift away from fossil fuels, and towards renewable energy sources and improved energy efficiency in products.

Scales of Production

Products are made using different methods of production. The method depends on the type of product being made and the quality and quantity demanded.

One-Off Production

In one-off production, bespoke products are made to meet specific customer requirements. Every product is unique.

Key Points

- One-off production is often labour intensive.

- It usually involves highly skilled workers who command relatively high wages.

- Each item is individually made so production can be time-consuming and costly. However, the finished product is usually of a high quality.

Examples: bespoke clothing, furniture and jewellery

A prototype is an early, working version of a product or system that is usually made using one-off production. It is used to test different aspects of a design and find ways to improve it.

Batch Production

In batch production, a set number of products are passed through the production process together, one stage at a time.

Key Points

- Batch production is useful when making small quantities of a product or variations of similar products.

- Machines can be programmed to carry out specific tasks, and the use of templates, jigs and moulds ensures that the products are identical.

- Machinery often has to be stopped and reconfigured for each batch. This is known as downtime. It can be inefficient, especially when lots of batches are required.

- Materials can be purchased in large quantities, enabling the business to benefit from economies of scale (lower unit costs when larger quantities are purchased).

Examples: a bakery making different types of bread or cake

daydream EDUCATION

Mass Production

In mass (or flow) production, the production process is broken down into stages, with different tasks being performed as the products move along the assembly line.

Key Points

- Mass production is used to produce large quantities of identical products quickly.

- Productivity is high, so unit cost of production is low. This allows the business to benefit from economies of scale and offer competitive prices.

- Workers or machines perform a simple dedicated task at each stage of the production process so little skilled labour is required.

- Machinery is costly so initial set-up is expensive.

Examples: newspapers, drinks bottles and cars

Continuous Production

In continuous production, identical products are made without interruption. Production will only stop occasionally for cleaning and maintenance, keeping downtime to a minimum.

Key Points

- Continuous production runs 24 hours a day, 7 days a week.

- Production is quick and almost entirely automated, so productivity is high and labour costs are low.

- Machinery is expensive, so initial set-up costs are high.

- Unit costs are very cheap due to economies of scale. However, because of the high level of automation, only a very limited range of products can be produced.

Examples: pulp and paper production, metal smelting and casting

Papers & Boards: Sources & Origins

Papers and boards are made from the **cellulose fibres** found in wood and some plants (grasses). They can also be made from recycled paper and board.

Making Paper and Board from Cellulose Fibres

1 Trees or grasses are cut down and transported to a paper mill.

2 Bark cannot be used in the paper-making process, so trees must be **debarked** before they can be processed.

The wood is then cut into fine chippings by a machine.

3 The chips or plants are mechanically or chemically **pulped** into individual cellulose fibres.

Chemical pulping involves cooking the woodchips under pressure in a chemical solution to remove lignin, which binds the cellulose fibres together.

4 The pulp is sent through filters, where bleach, additives and colourings are added to give the pulp its required finish.

5 The pulp is pressed between rollers to squeeze out excess water and to flatten it into long rolls of paper to be cut to size.

Recycled Paper and Board

Recycling paper and board reduces the need to cut down trees. It is also much more energy efficient to produce paper from recycled materials than from virgin pulp. Therefore, recycled paper and board is more environmentally friendly and sustainable than non-recycled paper.

However, there is a limit to how many times paper and board can be recycled.

daydream EDUCATION

Papers & Boards: Properties

The physical and mechanical properties of different types of paper and board make them suited for various commercial uses.

Flyers and Leaflets

Flyers and leaflets are used in advertising. The type of paper used for flyers and leaflets often depends on the product, event or business being advertised.

Bleed-proof, gloss paper is perfect for low-cost flyers and leaflets that require clear, sharp and colourful images.

Sometimes businesses will use more expensive, heavier and thicker paper when promoting luxury or high-cost items.

Most flyers are biodegradable.

Food Packaging

Different types of paper and board are suited to different types of food packaging. However, all food packaging should be non-toxic, lightweight and easily disposable.

If left untreated, most cardboard is absorbent. Therefore, it must be treated or coated with another material, such as plastic, before it can be used in food packaging. However, this can make it more difficult to dispose of.

Corrugated card is sturdy and good at retaining heat, making it ideal for takeaway pizza boxes.

Modifying the Properties of Paper and Boards

The properties of paper and boards can be enhanced by using additives. For example, some chemicals are used to help to prevent moisture transfer.

Sizing is a process that is performed during paper manufacture to provide a protective filler or coating. It reduces the absorbency of the paper so that the ink dries on the surface of the paper rather than seeping through, resulting in a brighter, clearer finish. Sizing is used in the manufacture of paper and boards that are used for packaging foods that must be kept dry, such as flour.

Parchment paper is made by running sheets of paper pulp through sulfuric acid. This gives it a non-stick surface.

Tissue paper contains wet-strength additives so that it retains its strength when it gets wet.

Kraft paper is strong and has a high resistance to tearing due to the chemicals and processes used during pulping.

Papers & Boards: Stock Forms, Types & Sizes

When designing a product, designers must consider the stock forms and sizes available. Stock forms and sizes are produced in bulk and therefore help to save on material costs.

Stock Forms

Paper and boards are available in three stock forms:

Sheet	**Roll**	**Ply (Layered)**
Common use: Art supplies	**Common use:** Newspaper printing	**Common use:** Kitchen roll

Stock Sizes

The A-series is part of the international paper size standard ISO 216.

A0 841 × 1189

594 594
420
A2 420 × 594
841 841
A1 594 × 841
297 297
210
A4 297 × 210
420
A3 297 × 420
148 148
105
A6 105 × 148
210
A5 148 × 210
A8 52 × 74
A7 74 × 105
A9 A10
1189

All measurements are in millimetres (mm)

A0 is the largest size, and the dimensions of sheets halve as you move down a size.

For example, A1 is half the size of A0, A2 is half the size of A1 and so on.

A4 and A3 are the sizes most commonly used in schools and offices.

Paper is also sold in different thicknesses, weights and colours. Paper weight is measured in grams per square metre (gsm). Anything up to and including 200 gsm is considered paper, and anything above 200 gsm is board.

daydream EDUCATION

Components, Seals and Bindings

There is a range of standard components that can be used with paper and boards.

Paperclips

Metal fasteners used to loosely hold together a small number of sheets of paper

Binder Clips

Spring clips used to temporarily hold together a number of sheets of paper

Split Pins

Pins with flexible ends used as joints to hold paper together

Staples

Small pieces of metal that are punched through paper to hold them together semi-permanently

Treasury Tags

Simple fasteners that are placed through punched holes to hold paper together loosely

Bindings are used to hold together a larger quantity of paper. For example, the paper in a book or a large document such as a university dissertation.

Slide Binding

A simple piece of plastic is slid onto the side of the sheets of paper.

Comb Binding

A 'comb' is punched through the paper using a binding machine.

Coil (Spiral) Binding

A coil is inserted through punched holes in the paper.

Perfect Binding

Pages are folded in sections and glued to the spine of the book. The book will not open flat.

Saddle Stitch

Pages are stapled together at the centre of the book.

Section-Sewn Binding

Pages are folded in sections and sewn to the spine of the book. The book can open flat.

Seals are used to bond pieces of paper and card.

Gummed Envelopes

Envelopes with an adhesive strip that must be moistened and pressed to seal

Peel-and-Seal Envelopes

Envelopes with a strip that must be peeled off to expose the adhesive

Wax Seals

An old method of sealing where hot wax is applied and dried to seal the paper

Adhesives (e.g. glue sticks, spray adhesives and liquid glues) and tapes (e.g. double-sided tape and duct tape) are also used to bond paper and card.

Papers & Boards: Shaping & Forming

Papers and boards can be **cut, creased, scored, folded** and **perforated** to achieve a desired shape or form.

Cutting & Perforating

There are various tools available to cut and perforate paper and card.

Scissors

Scissors are the most commonly used everyday cutting tool.

They are good for basic cutting but are not well-suited to intricate or refined cutting work.

Craft Knives

Craft knives are used with safety rulers to cut and score material.

They are available in many different forms and are particularly good for making straight cuts.

Scalpels

Scalpels have small, sharp and thin blades that are ideal for cutting intricate details.

The blades are replaceable, so they can be kept sharp.

Rotary Cutters

Rotary cutters use a circular blade that rotates to cut paper and card.

They are good for curved cuts.

Perforating Tools

Perforating tools punch small holes through paper to allow it to be easily torn.

Perforating can be done by using rotary handheld perforating tools, die cutters and laser cutters.

Guillotines

Guillotines, or paper trimmers, are used to cut sheets of paper with a straight edge.

They are often used to cut large sheets of paper.

Laser Cutters

Laser cutters use lasers to cut intricate patterns into paper and card.

The lasers burn through the material to provide extremely accurate and fine cuts.

Compass Cutters

Compass cutters can be used to cut perfect arcs and circles in paper and card.

daydream EDUCATION

Scoring

Scoring involves partially cutting into a material without going all the way through, usually to aid folding. It is often performed before folding thick paper or board that would otherwise be difficult to fold.

Scoring can be done by hand using a craft knife and a metal ruler. It is important to press lightly when running the knife along the score line, so that the blade does not cut all the way through.

Scoring results in straighter, more accurate folds.

Folding

Paper and board can be folded along creases or scored lines.

Some items, such as wine boxes, can be folded by hand from pre-cut material. These are creased ready for easy assembly and can be stored flat when not in use to save space. Origami is a Japanese craft where paper is folded into intricate shapes, such as animals and geometric shapes. One of the most well-known origami structures is the crane.

Sometimes, specialist folding machines will be used to fold large quantities of items quickly and accurately. This is often done with mass-produced commercial items, such as supermarket cereal boxes.

Die Cutting

Die cutters are used to cut, crease or perforate paper to create shapes and make nets.

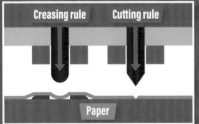

Creasing rule   **Cutting rule**

Paper

Die cutters use a die (which works like a cookie cutter) to cut or crease material into a specific shape. A sharp blade is used where a cut is required, and a round edge is used where a crease is required.

The die is uniquely shaped to match the shape of the desired design, so when it is pressed against the paper, the paper is cut and creased in the correct places.

There are various forms of die cutter available, including large-scale industrial presses that can mass-produce cut-out shapes and nets for use in 3D packaging, such as postage boxes.

Although the initial cost of metal dies can be expensive, die cutting is very accurate and allows identical shapes to be cut quickly and to a high standard.

Papers & Boards: Surface Treatments & Finishes

Adding a special finish to papers and boards can improve the way they look as well as their functionality. For example, laminating a poster can make it water-resistant for use outdoors.

Printing

Printing is the main finishing process used for paper and boards.

Colour Printing

There are two main methods for colour printing. Both methods involve combining different quantities of base colours to create different colours and shades.

 The RGB colour mode uses three base colours (red, green and blue) to make all other colours.

 The CMYK colour mode uses four base colours to make all other colours; cyan, magenta, yellow and key (black).

Offset Lithography

Offset lithography is based on the principle that oil and water do not mix.

1 An image is applied to an aluminium printing plate using UV light.

2 The plate is chemically treated so that the blank area attracts water and the image attracts oil-based ink.

3 The plate is attached to a plate cylinder, and water and ink are applied to this with water and ink rollers.

4 The image picks up the ink, and the blank area picks up the water.

5 The plate cylinder presses against a blanket cylinder, which presses away excess water and transfers the ink image to a piece of paper.

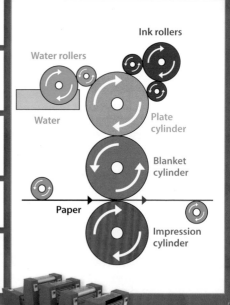

Ink rollers

Water rollers

Water

Plate cylinder

Blanket cylinder

Paper

Impression cylinder

Offset lithography uses four colours (CMYK). It is used for items with long print runs such as newspapers, magazines and books.

daydream EDUCATION

Printing (continued)

Screen Printing

Screen printing is a simple process that is ideal for short runs and for prints that do not require a high level of detail (e.g. posters).

1 A stencil is placed below a mesh screen, and the paper is placed below it.

2 Ink is spread over the mesh screen using a rubber squeegee.

3 The ink is transferred through the stencil and onto the paper to print the design.

Flexography

In flexography, the image or text is raised into a relief on the printing plate. It works on many different materials, not just paper and boards.

- It can be used for high volumes of print and is quick compared to other forms of printing. The ink is also quick-drying.

- The plates can be reused multiple times if well-maintained.

- The initial cost of flexography plates is high, and setting up can be time-consuming.

Gravure

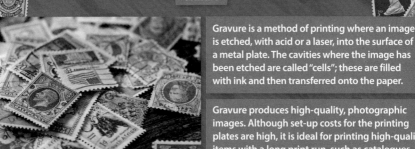

Gravure is a method of printing where an image is etched, with acid or a laser, into the surface of a metal plate. The cavities where the image has been etched are called "cells"; these are filled with ink and then transferred onto the paper.

Gravure produces high-quality, photographic images. Although set-up costs for the printing plates are high, it is ideal for printing high-quality items with a long print run, such as catalogues and brochures, and those with fine detail, such as stamps and printed photographs.

Gravure printing allows for a high-quality finish, even where low-quality paper has been used.

Other Finishes

Embossing

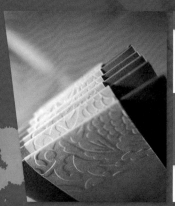

Embossing involves pressing a specially shaped die onto the surface of a material to create a raised image. Although expensive, embossing can add a high-quality finish to luxury paper and card products.

To emboss a design onto paper, the sheet is placed between a custom-made counter die (or 'male' die) and a relief die (or 'female' die). The paper is compressed between the dies, and pressure or heat is applied. When the dies are released, a raised design remains on the paper.

Embossing is also useful for making Braille labels on medicines to help the visually impaired.

Laminating

Lamination is used to protect paper and card from damage and wear. It can have a shiny or matt finish and is commonly used for posters, menus and membership cards.

A laminating machine is used to press a sheet of paper or card between a plastic sleeve. Heated rollers inside the machine press the sleeve and paper together and bond them with heat. As the paper is pulled between the rollers, the plastic film is sealed around it.

Lamination can also be applied cold or by using liquid.

Varnishing

Varnishing is commonly used to add a shiny or matt surface finish either to a whole sheet of paper or just one specific area (spot varnishing). Varnishing can be done during or after the printing process.

UV Varnishing

UV varnishing protects paper from wear. It is commonly used for products such as glossy magazines, business cards and brochures. It involves applying a varnish to the paper and then drying it under a UV light.

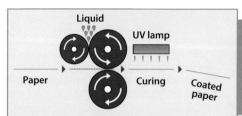

Drying the varnish under a UV light makes it a much quicker process than standard varnishing. Under UV, the varnish dries instantly. This makes it ideal for food packaging, which may need to be folded immediately.

daydream
EDUCATION

Timbers: Sources & Origins

Wood from trees can be converted into different forms of natural timber and manufactured boards.

Wood is the raw material used for timber-based materials. There are two main types.

Hardwood
from deciduous trees

Oak Tree

- Maple
- Teak
- Oak
- Mahogany
- Redwood
- Balsa
- Larch

Softwood
from coniferous trees

Pine Trees

- Spruce
- Pine
- Yew

Hardwood tends to take longer to mature before it can be felled (cut down). Therefore, it takes longer to replace and is generally more expensive.

Conversion

After being felled, tree trunks are stripped of their bark and cut into usable planks in a sawmill, where they become timber. Planks come in many different shapes and sizes.

A plank's cut affects its risk of warping or twisting, as well as its cost. The more complex the cut, the costlier the timber. For example, quarter cut wood is more expensive than baulk cut.

Through and Through Cut

- Cost-effective and quick
- Can warp and twist easily
- General use

Quarter Cut

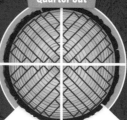

- Complex and expensive
- Creates a lot of waste
- High-quality cut
- Used in high-quality furniture

Baulk Cut

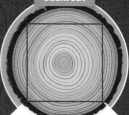

- Very simple cut
- Not very versatile
- Used in posts and beams

Planks can be **rough-sawn** or **planed all round (PAR)**. PAR planks are planed for a smooth finish and are therefore more suitable for use where a quality finish is required.

Seasoning

Newly cut (green) timber contains a lot of moisture, which makes it liable to rot, split and warp. To counteract this, the moisture is removed through seasoning.

Air Seasoning

Timber can be seasoned naturally through air seasoning.

Planks are stacked under a roofed, unwalled shelter and separated by stickers (thin pieces of wood) to allow air to circulate between the planks. Air seasoning is cost-effective but takes a long time. For example, it takes around a year to dry 25 mm planks of wood.

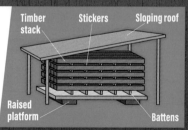

Kiln Seasoning

Kiln seasoning is carried out in the same way as air seasoning, but heat, steam and pressure are used to speed up the drying process. The moisture in the kiln is reduced gradually to avoid damage to the timber.

Kiln seasoning is faster but more expensive than air seasoning.

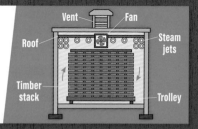

Manufactured Boards

Wood can be processed into manufactured boards, which are made from fibres, chips, blocks or sheets of wood bonded together with adhesives.

Plywood

Alternate layers of wood (veneers) are glued together at 90 degrees to each other.

Medium-Density Fibreboard (MDF)

Woodchips are broken down into a pulp (small fibres), mixed with glue and compressed.

Chipboard

Small chips of wood are compressed and glued together.

Manufactured boards are often created from waste or recycled materials.

daydream EDUCATION

Timbers: Properties

Different types of wood have varying properties (e.g. strength, hardness, durability) that make them suited for different purposes and commercial products. In addition to considering the properties of wood, designers must also consider how easy the materials are to manufacture.

Wooden Toys

Wooden toys need to be durable to withstand being thrown, hit and dropped. Furthermore, small children are likely to chew on toys, so the material should also be hard enough not to splinter easily and cause harm to the child.

Hardwoods, such as beech and oak, are commonly used for toys because of their hardness and durability.
They are also easy to paint and unlikely to break into small parts that may pose choking hazards.

Flat-Pack Furniture

Manufactured boards are commonly used in flat-pack furniture. They are cheaper than natural wood furniture and are easy to assemble and disassemble again for transportation. They can also be finished with various veneers to achieve different looks.

Veneers give the appearance of a quality piece of furniture, but at a significantly reduced price when compared to the solid wood equivalent.

Flat-pack furniture is generally not as strong or durable as solid wood furniture. It is also prone to moisture damage which, if affected, can cause difficulty with assembly.

The absence of any grain, and the consistency of the small wood particles, make manufactured boards easy to machine and work with.

Modification of Timber-Based Materials

Wood is seasoned to alter its moisture content and to create properties suited to its intended use. For example, reducing the moisture content of wood can make it stronger and less likely to rot. However, unseasoned wood is cheaper and easier to shape.

Timbers: Stock Forms, Types & Sizes

Timber is available in a range of stock forms and sizes to suit different purposes.

Planks, Boards & Strips

Timber planks, boards and strips are available in a range of stock sizes, with set lengths, widths and thicknesses. Measurements are usually listed as **length × width × thickness (mm)**.

Planed Timber

Timber is available rough-cut and planed. Planed timber is smoother than rough-cut timber, but it is also more expensive.

Planing removes around 2–3 mm of material from each side of the timber, so planed timber is slightly smaller than rough-cut timber.

Rough-cut Timber

Mouldings

Mouldings are specially shaped sections of wood that are commonly used for frames, architraves (moulded frames around doorways and windows) and skirting boards.

Dowels are cylindrical timber rods that come in a range of diameters. They are used to join pieces of wood together, often in furniture.

Manufactured Boards

Manufactured boards are most commonly available in standard 2400 × 1220-mm sheets. However, various smaller sizes are also available.

The thickness of manufactured boards varies and generally increases in 3-mm increments (e.g. 6 mm, 9 mm, 12 mm).

Standard Components - Screws

Woodscrews are used to temporarily join two pieces of wood together.
They are available in different lengths and diameters and are usually made from brass or steel.
They also have different shaped heads for different applications.

 Slotted

 Pozidriv

 Phillips

 Allen (hexagonal)

58

daydream EDUCATION

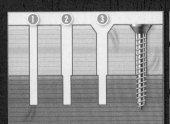

1 Drill a pilot hole through both pieces of wood. This hole should be slightly narrower than the thread of the screw.

2 Drill a clearance hole through the top piece of wood. This hole should be slightly larger than the shank or thread of the screw.

3 If using a countersunk screw, a countersunk hole should be drilled to the depth of the screw.

Self-drilling screws that negate the need for pilot and clearance holes are also available. They have a sharp end (like a drill bit) and a tapered thread to create a hole.

Standard Components - Hinges

Hinges are used to allow doors, windows and lids to open and close. They are commonly made from brass, steel or plastic and are fixed to the wood with screws.

Butt Hinge

The most common type of hinge for windows and doors, a butt hinge is usually recessed into the surfaces.

Flush Hinge

It works like a butt hinge but is screwed directly onto the wood. It is easier to position but not as strong.

Concealed Hinge

Commonly used inside cabinets, a concealed hinge is easily adjustable but often needs to be recessed into one of the surfaces.

Hinges are also used on plastic and metal windows and doors.

Standard Components - Knock-Down Fittings

Knock-down (KD) fittings are joints that are often used in the assembly of flat-pack furniture. They allow quick assembly and disassembly, but they are not as strong as permanent joints. They are usually assembled using simple tools such as screwdrivers and hex keys.

Corner Block Fitting

Corner block

A corner block is placed in the corner where two pieces of wood join at 90°. Screws are then screwed through ready-made holes to hold the block fitting and two pieces of wood in position.

Cam Lock

Peg

Cam nut

A disk (cam) is placed into a pre-drilled slot in one piece of wood, and a peg is inserted into the other. The peg slots into the side of the cam, and as the cam is turned, it grips the peg pulling the two pieces of wood together.

Scan Fitting

Barrel nut

Screw

Also known as a cross-dowel fitting, a barrel with a screw thread (barrel nut) is placed into a pre-drilled hole in one piece of wood, and a screw is placed in the other. The screw is then tightened, pulling the two pieces of wood together.

Timbers: Surface Treatments & Finishes

Treatments and finishes are applied to timbers to improve their appearance and to enhance certain properties, such as durability.

Painting

Paint is used to change the colour of wood and to add protection. It is applied using brushes, rollers or aerosol sprays. Before painting, wood must be properly prepared. This includes:

Cleaning and sanding the wood to provide a smooth, clean surface.

Priming the wood with a preparatory coating helps seal the wood so the paint sticks to the surface better.

An undercoat must also be applied before the top coat. This masks any previous colours and helps the top coat stick. A thinner, less expensive paint is usually used for the undercoat.

Oil-based paints are hard-wearing and water-resistant but take a long time to dry, whereas water-based paints are not very durable but are easy to work with and dry quickly.

Polyurethane paints harden when exposed to air, which makes them very durable.

Varnishing

Varnish is translucent and provides a hard, protective finish to wood.

Many types of wood have an attractive grain, so varnish is used instead of paint so the grain can be seen. Between each coat of varnish, the surface of the wood should be sanded lightly.

Varnish is available in matt, satin and gloss finishes. Varnishes that contain polyurethane are used to protect surfaces against heat and moisture and are commonly used on interior wood.

Tanalising

Preservatives can be added to wood through a process called tanalising. This protects the wood from rot, decay and insects to give it a longer life when used outside.

① Wood is placed into a tank, and a vacuum is created by drawing out all the air.

② The tank is flooded with a preservative treatment.

③ Pressure is applied, forcing the preservative deep into the wood.

④ Excess preservative is drained from the tank, and the wood is left out to dry.

daydream
EDUCATION

Metals: Sources & Origins

Most metals are found in ores within the Earth's crust. They must be **extracted** and **refined** before they can be used to make products.

Extracting Metals

Metals can be extracted from their ores, but the extraction method used depends on the metal's properties.

Furnace Heating

Metals can be extracted from their ores in a blast furnace. The ore is heated to such a high temperature that the metal separates from the other substances in the ore.

For example, iron is extracted from iron ore by heating the ore to a temperature above the iron's melting point. This causes the iron to melt and separate from the rest of the ore.

Metals can also be extracted from their ores using electrolysis. This involves passing an electrical current through the ore to separate the metal from the other substances in the ore.

A huge amount of energy is needed, so electrolysis is very expensive. It is used to extract aluminium from aluminium oxide, and it is also used in refining.

Refining Metals

Metals extracted from their ores often contain impurities. To obtain a pure metal, any impurities must be separated from the metal through a process called **refining**.

Distillation

The metal is heated to its boiling point, so it evaporates, leaving behind any impurities with higher boiling points. The pure metal then cools and condenses. Distillation is used with metals with low boiling points such as zinc and mercury.

Liquation

The metal is heated to its melting point and melts, while any impurities with higher melting points remain solid. As the metal melts, it runs away where it is collected in its pure state. Liquation is used with metals such as tin and lead.

Metals: Properties

Metals have varying properties (e.g. strength, hardness, toughness, malleability) that make them suited for different purposes and commercial products. However, as well as considering the properties of the product it is also important to consider cost, availability and the environment.

Cooking Utensils

Stainless steel is commonly used in cooking utensils because it is:

- Durable
- Dishwasher-safe
- Flame- and heat-resistant
- Resistant to rust and corrosion
- Aesthetically pleasing
- Safe to use with food

Although stainless steel is a popular choice for utensils, it is a relatively poor conductor of heat. To compensate for this, utensils often have a copper or aluminium core.

Hand Tools

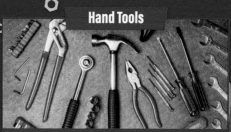

High-carbon (tool) steel is often used to make hand tools because it is:

- Strong
- Tough
- Resistant to abrasion
- Malleable
- Able to retain its shape, even at very high temperatures

Steel is available in a range of grades to suit different purposes. The amount of carbon and other elements in steel affects its properties. For example, chromium is added to steel to increase its resistance to corrosion.

Modifying the Properties of Metals

Properties of metals can be modified through heating and cooling.

Medium- and high-carbon steel can be hardened through heating and rapid cooling (quenching), but this also makes it brittle.

Annealing is a process that softens metal to make it more malleable and ductile so that it can be worked on again. It involves heating the metal to a specific temperature and then allowing it to cool slowly.

The process can be carried out repeatedly whenever the metal becomes hard and brittle again.

daydream
EDUCATION

Metals: Stock Forms, Types & Sizes

Stock Forms & Sizes

When creating a metal product, designers must consider the stock forms available because metals can be difficult and costly to manufacture in custom-made forms. Common stock forms include:

Sheet **Rod** **Flat Strip** **Tube**

Angle **Channel** **Strip**

Metals are available in various lengths, widths, thicknesses and diameters. Measurements are usually given in millimetres (mm).

Metal wire is measured by standard wire gauge (swg). The lower the **gauge**, the bigger the size. For example, 14 swg is equivalent to 2.03 mm and 12 swg is equivalent to 2.64 mm.

Wire gauge tools can be used to measure swg values.

Standard Components

There are a range of standard components that can be used with metals.

Rivets

Rivets are used to join pieces (usually sheets) of metal.

Rivets can be installed manually using a hammer. The rivet is inserted through a pre-drilled hole in both materials so the head of the rivet is flush against the one side. The other end of the rivet on the other side of the material is then shaped into a head using a hammer.

daydream EDUCATION

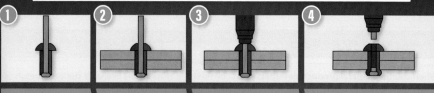

Pop Rivets

Pop rivets are useful when only one side of the metal can be accessed.

① A pin is inserted through the centre of the rivet.

② The rivet is then inserted into the hole.

③ A rivet gun is then used to pull the pin with enough force to cause it to snap off.

④ The force of the pin being pulled up deforms the end of the rivet, creating a head on the other side.

Rivet heads are available in a range of shapes and sizes depending on their function.

Rivets are commonly used in aeroplanes and bridges.

Machine Screws

Machine screws are used to temporarily join parts together.

In contrast to tapered screws, which narrow to a point, they have a uniform diameter along the entire length of the shank. Therefore, they can only be used with a nut and washer or in a hole that matches the size of the thread.

Machine screws are available with different head shapes (e.g. countersunk) and driving methods, and in different widths and lengths.

 Slotted   **Pozidriv**   **Phillips**   **Allen** (hexagonal)

Nuts and Bolts

A nut is a metal fastener with a threaded hole, and a bolt is a type of screw that fits the thread in the nut. Nuts and bolts are used to join materials together, including wood, metal and plastic.

Nuts and bolts are usually made from carbon steel, but some are coated with zinc to make them resistant to corrosion that can occur when they are used outdoors (e.g. in bridges).

Bolt heads are usually square or hexagonal shaped so they can be tightened with tools such as spanners or socket wrenches.

A nyloc nut contains a nylon collar insert. When tightened on a bolt, the nylon insert deforms elastically around the bolt. This locks the nut in place and provides increased grip. Nyloc nuts are less prone to leaking and loosening due to vibration.

Washers are often used with machine screws and nuts and bolts to spread the load and prevent loosening.

Metals: Surface Treatments & Finishes

Metals are susceptible to damage through **corrosion**, which occurs as a result of chemical reactions between the metal and the surrounding environment. Adding surface treatments and finishes such as paint can help protect metal and improve its appearance.

Before treatments or finishes are added to a metal, it is first **smoothed** and **cleaned** with abrasives (e.g. metal wool) and chemical cleaners (e.g. degreaser).

Dip Coating

Dip coating involves covering a metal with a thin layer of plastic.

The metal is heated to 180–200°C and then dipped into fluidised plastic powder (powder that has air blown through it to make it act like a liquid).

The coated metal is returned to the oven, and the fluidised plastic remaining on the metal now melts and sticks to the surface to give a smooth, shiny finish.

Dip coating is often used to cover tool handles and wheelchair parts.

Powder Coating

Powder coating involves spraying plastic powder onto a metal part and heating it.

The dry powder spray is applied with an electrostatic gun, which gives the spray an electrical charge. The metal part has the opposite charge, which attracts the spray and allows it to stick.

The coated metal is then heated in an oven to fuse the powder to the metal surface. It is then left to cool, forming a hard coating.

The use of electrostatic charge allows coatings to be applied to even the most complex shapes and ensures a smooth, even finish. It is commonly used for wheels, bike frames and outdoor play equipment.

Galvanising

Galvanising is a process used to protect a base metal such as iron or steel from corrosion. This is done by coating the base metal with a more reactive metal, such as zinc.

The zinc forms a barrier over the base metal that protects it from moisture and oxygen, which cause corrosion. However, if the barrier is scratched deeply enough, the base metal can become exposed.

Hot-dip galvanising involves submerging the base metal entirely in molten zinc. Gates and metal pails are often galvanised.

Polymers: Sources & Origins

Most plastics are man-made polymers that are synthesised from crude oil.

Refining Crude Oil

Crude oil is made up of a large number of hydrocarbon molecules that are not very useful when combined. As a result, they are separated and refined into more useful products. This is done through a process called **fractional distillation.**

Fractional Distillation

Fractional distillation involves separating the hydrocarbons in crude oil into fractions. This is done in a fractionating column. Fractional distillation works on the basis that each fraction:

- Has a different boiling point
- Condenses at a different temperature

The fractions condense at different points in the fractionating column, with each one being used for a different purpose.

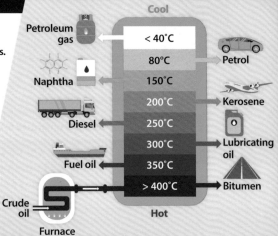

Cool

Petroleum gas	< 40°C
	80°C — Petrol
Naphtha	150°C
	200°C — Kerosene
Diesel	250°C
	300°C — Lubricating oil
Fuel oil	350°C
	> 400°C — Bitumen

Crude oil — Furnace

Hot

Cracking

Before the separated fractions can be used to manufacture polymers, they need to be broken down further into monomers by a process called **cracking.**

During cracking, the fractions are heated to break them down into individual hydrocarbons, including ethylene and propylene, which can then be used to manufacture polymers.

Polymerisation

$$C=C$$

Ethylene molecule

Polyethylene chain

To complete the manufacture of polymers, monomers must be joined together to make longer polymer chains. This process is known as **polymerisation**. In the example, ethylene monomers have been joined together to form polyethylene.

daydream EDUCATION

Polymers: Properties

Plastics have different properties (strength, toughness, durability and insulation) that make them suitable for different commercial uses. When choosing plastics, it is also important to consider cost, availability, ease of manufacture and the environment.

Polymer Seating

Thermoplastics, such as polypropylene, have properties that make them ideal for use in seats.

Polypropylene is tough and lightweight with a good strength-to-weight ratio. Therefore, it can easily withstand the pressure of a person's weight. It is also easily coloured and moulded into different shapes, so it can be designed to suit a range of styles and purposes.

Because the material is waterproof and resistant to corrosion and chemicals, it can be used in school, dining and outdoor environments.

Electrical Fittings

Thermosetting plastics are usually more brittle and rigid than thermoplastics. However, they are good electrical insulators and resistant to heat and fire.

Urea formaldehyde is a hard electrical insulator that is also heat- and fire-resistant. This makes it ideal for use in electrical fittings because it does not melt when exposed to extreme heat. Therefore, it stops the spread of fire in case of an electrical fault and prevents electrical shocks.

Modification of Polymers

Polymers are often blended with additives to improve certain properties.

For example, UV light from the Sun and artificial lighting can damage the chemical structure of polymers, causing them to become weaker and more brittle. Coloured polymers will also fade and take on a 'powdered' look.

To prevent UV degradation, plastic products are often treated with stabilisers that absorb the UV radiation and emit it as heat. This prevents the UV light from altering the chemical structure.

Other additives include plasticisers, which increase flexibility, and flame retardants, which inhibit the production of flames and prevent the spread of fire.

Polymers: Stock Forms, Types & Sizes

Stock Forms & Sizes

Plastics are available in the following stock forms:

Sheet

Uses: Line bending, signage, roofing, vacuum forming

Rod & Tubes

Uses: Machining, curtain parts

Foam

Uses: Packaging, seating, flotation aids

Film

Uses: Food packaging, vacuum forming

Granules

Uses: Injection moulding, casting

Powder

Uses: Dip coating, spray coating, 3D printing

Plastics are available in various **lengths, widths, thicknesses** and **diameters** (for round cross-sections). Measurements are usually given in millimetres (**mm**): length × width × thickness.

Thickness is also measured by gauge, and powder and granules are measured by weight (g).

Standard Components

Many of the components made from woods and metals are also made from plastics. Although metal components are generally strongest, plastic components are usually favoured on items where rust and corrosion are an issue. For added strength, plastic components with metal cores can be used.

Machine Screws

Machine screws are used to temporarily join parts together.

They have a uniform diameter along the entire length of the shank, as opposed to tapered screws, which narrow to a point.

They are available with different head shapes (e.g. countersunk) and driving methods (e.g. Phillips) and in varying widths and lengths (measured in millimetres).

daydream EDUCATION

Nuts and Bolts

Nuts and bolts are used to join materials together, including wood, metal and plastic.

A nut is a fastener with a threaded hole, and a bolt is a type of screw which fits the thread in the nut. They have a range of different types and styles, but usually have a square or hexagonal head that can be tightened with tools such as spanners or socket wrenches.

Nuts and bolts are commonly made from carbon steel or are coated with zinc, but plastic varieties are also available. These include nylon, PVC and PET.

Plastic nuts and bolts are used in applications where their resistance to corrosion and lightweight properties are an added advantage. For example, their non-conductivity makes them ideal for electronic applications.

Unlike metal nuts and bolts, plastic varieties have an endless array of colours available.

Hinges

Hinges are used to allow objects to open and close. Plastic hinges are not as strong as metal varieties, but have the added advantage that they are lightweight and will not rust. This makes them ideal for outdoor applications that do not require a great deal of strength.

Butt hinge

Plastic butt hinges are commonly used for light-duty openings, furniture and cabinet doors with the added advantage that they do not corrode or require lubrication. They often contain a metal pin inside for added strength, though pinless varieties are also available.

Continuous hinge

Continuous hinges are used as an alternative to metal piano hinges. They are used for hatches and lids, with the added advantage that they do not corrode or require lubrication. They are usually cut to size.

Concealed hinge

Plastic concealed hinges are often used for openings such as kitchen cabinets to allow for silent use. They are fixed to the inside of the cabinet door so that they cannot be seen from the outside.

The plastic components shown above are typically made of **nylon**.

Polymers: Surface Treatments & Finishes

Plastics are usually self-finishing and do not require extra protection: they are already resistant to corrosion and rot. If a finish is added, it is generally for aesthetic purposes.

Polishing

If plastic has been cut to shape, it may have rough edges. To smooth these out, the edges are first filed. Then, the plastic is rubbed with abrasive paper, or a machine such as a **buffing wheel** can be used with a polishing compound to achieve a very high-quality finish. This can then be followed up with a final polish.

These techniques can be used to remove fine surface scratches.

Printing

Some of the main ways in which designs can be printed directly onto plastics include:

- Offset lithography
- Flexography
- Screen printing

For more information on each of these printing methods, please see 'Paper and Boards: Surface Treatments and Finishes'.

Heat transfer printing is another common method of printing on plastics. This involves applying a design to the surface of the plastic with a heat press.

A special film that contains a heat-sensitive adhesive on one side is used for transferring the design. When heat is applied, the adhesive then bonds to the plastic.

Vinyl Decals

A decal is a design used to decorate the surface of materials. The design is printed on a vinyl sheet with an adhesive coating on one side. It is then transferred to the surface of a material using heat or water.

Vinyl sheets are fed through a printer and cutter to print and shape the design for use. These designs are usually created with specialised computer software.

daydream EDUCATION

Timbers, Metals & Polymers: Shaping & Forming

Wood, metals and polymers can be shaped and formed through cutting, abrasion and addition using a variety of tools, equipment and processes.

Cutting

Wood, metals and polymers can be cut to size with a variety of tools.

Rip Saw / Cross-Cut Saw

Rip saws are used to cut parallel to the grain, whereas cross-cut saws are used to cut against the grain

Used to cut **wood**

Tenon Saw

Cuts accurate straight lines in small pieces of wood and provides a smooth cut

Used to cut **wood**

Hacksaw

Has a hard, high-carbon steel blade so it can cut through metal; also available in a junior size for smaller cuts

Used to cut **metal** and **plastic**

Coping Saw

Can cut intricate curves in thin materials but is difficult to control; has a blade that can snap easily

Used to cut **wood** and **plastic**

When cutting materials, follow the steps outlined below.

1 Secure the material with a clamp, or by placing it in a vice to prevent it from moving while the material is being cut.

2 Make a mark in the material you want to cut by dragging the saw backwards a few times; this will provide you with a guide to start sawing.

3 Use the full length of the blade when sawing, and don't press down too hard. Let the blade do the work!

4 When coming to the end of the cut, support the end piece to stop it from falling off and spoiling the cut.

Jigsaw

A jigsaw is a handheld power tool that is used to make straight or curved cuts. Blades are interchangeable, so it can be used to cut wood, metal and plastic.

Band Saw

A band saw is a machine tool that is used to make straight and curved cuts in wood, but can also be used to thin wood into sheet. Blades can be changed to cut soft metals and plastics.

Router

A router is a power tool that is used to cut decorative edges, grooves and shapes into wood. Handheld and larger machine types are available.

Drilling

Drills are used to make holes in materials. A trigger is pulled, which turns on an electric motor and causes the attached drill bit to rotate. The drill bit is then pressed against the target material to make a hole.

Power Drill

Power drills can be used with a wide variety of drill bits to drill holes in woods, plastics and metals. Cordless forms are available that are more portable than corded versions, but they are generally not as powerful.

Pillar Drill

Different drill bits can be attached to the pillar drill to drill holes of various types and sizes. Pillar drills have far more accuracy than cordless drills and can drill bigger holes through harder materials.

Drill Bits

Drill bits are available in a wide range of sizes and types. It is important to select the correct drill bit for the desired job based on the target material and the size and depth of the required hole.

Flat Bit

Used to drill large, deep, flat-bottomed holes in wood and plastic

Twist Bit

Used to drill small holes in wood, metals and plastics

Countersink Bit

Used to make holes for countersunk screw heads and bolts

Forstner Bit

Used with pillar drills to drill large, flat-bottomed holes

A lip and spur drill bit is a type of twist bit that can be used on wood. It contains a drill point to help keep the bit still for accurate drilling.

Center Punch

Sometimes, it helps to mark the target materials with a bradawl (wood) or a centre punch (metal). The mark guides the drill bit into the correct place for drilling.

Bradawl

Safety tip: It is important to select the right drill speed to prevent overheating (the bigger the drill bit, the slower the speed). The material should also be clamped down firmly.

daydream
EDUCATION

Chiselling

Chisels are used to cut or shape wood (special types are also used to cut or shape stone and metal). They are long-bladed, bevel-edged hand tools that are struck with a hammer or mallet to remove material. Chiselling involves forcing the blade into the target material to carve or cut it.

Safety tip: When chiselling, ensure that the blade is sharp and that the wood is securely held in place.

Planing, Sanding & Filing

Materials can be shaped through planing, filing and sanding.

Planing

Planing is used to shape and smooth material (usually wood). It involves shaving off thin layers of the material until the desired shape and feel are achieved.

Manual hand planers and electric planers are available. Electric planers are quick and require much less effort than manual hand planers, but they are not as accurate.

Sanding

Sanding involves rubbing an abrasive paper against the surface of the material to shape and smooth it. It can be performed by hand or using machines.

Sandpaper is available in different grades. Coarse paper is ideal for heavy sanding and stripping. Conversely, extremely fine sandpaper is used for smoothing a surface and removing small imperfections.

Different versions, such as wet and dry paper, are also available for different materials. This type of sandpaper is ideal for removing paint from painted metal and wood.

Belt Sander

This is a powerful machine used to smooth wood, metals and plastics more quickly and effectively than hand sanding. It contains a motor that drives a pair of drums on which a belt of abrasive paper is held.

Disc Sander

This is a machine that has a powered disc of abrasive paper that is spun at high speed. It smooths surfaces and removes old finishes (e.g. paint) when wood, metals or plastics are pressed up against it.

Safety tip: Sanders create a lot of dust, so dust extractors must be switched on to reduce the risk of fire and inhalation. Goggles must also be worn to protect the eyes, and fingers should be kept away from abrasive materials on power sanders.

daydream EDUCATION

Filing

Files have a serrated (toothed) surface so when they are rubbed over a material, some of the target material is removed. They can be used on a variety of materials and are available in different forms.

Files with larger teeth remove more material than those with smaller teeth, which are better suited for smoothing.

Turning

Materials such as wood and metal can be shaped using a **lathe**.

Lathes are machines that spin, or turn, a material at varying **speeds**. As the material spins, a wood-turning chisel is **pressed** against it to remove material.

Common items made by wood turning include chair legs, table legs and bowls.

Some lathes use computer numerical control (CNC) to shape **materials**. The machine executes pre-programmed sequences of commands to shape the material.

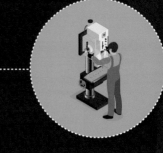

Milling

Milling machines use rotary cutters to remove material. They are versatile machines that can be used to drill, bore, machine edges, cut grooves and smooth surfaces. They are primarily used with metals but can also be used with wood and plastics.

There are two main types of milling machine:

Vertical Mills	The spindle axis is positioned vertically.	Horizontal Mills	The spindle axis is positioned horizontally.

Different bits can be added to carry out different tasks.

Some milling machines use CNC to shape materials. The machine executes pre-programmed sequences of commands to shape the material.

daydream
EDUCATION

Soldering, Brazing & Welding

Soldering, brazing and welding are processes that permanently join materials together.

Soldering

Soldering involves joining metal with a filler (usually an alloy of lead and tin) that has a relatively low melting point.

The filler is melted using a soldering iron and applied to the parts that are to be joined. It is used to attach components to circuit boards.

Brazing

Brazing is carried out at a higher temperature than soldering and lower temperature than welding.

Before the metal is joined, it is cleaned, and flux is added to prevent oxidation. The joint is heated, and a brazing rod of a different metal is then melted against it. It is then left to cool slowly and solidify the joint.

Welding

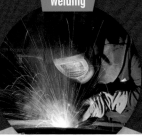

Welding is the strongest way to join metal or plastics. Unlike soldering and brazing, it melts the base material and the filler.

Heat is applied to the materials at the joint to melt and fuse them together. A welding rod is used to strengthen the joint. Solvents are used to weld plastics by temporarily dissolving them.

3D Printing

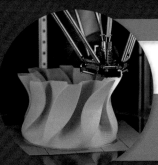

3D printing is a form of 'additional manufacturing' in which thin layers of thermoplastic are used to build a physical object from a digital design. This is achieved through CAD/CAM technology.

Some 3D printers are available that can print with other materials, such as metal and ceramics.

It is hoped that in the future, it will be possible to produce food and even human body parts using 3D printers.

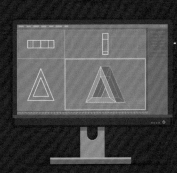

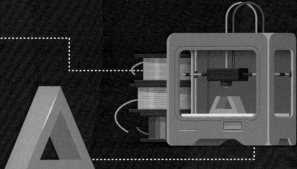

Lamination

Bending Wood

In wood lamination, thin sheets of wood, or **veneers**, are glued together in layers. This adds strength and can be used to create bent and curved wooden boards.

To bend the wood, layers of wood are glued and then clamped into the desired position in a former or jig. When the glue is completely dry, the wood is removed and retains its shape.

Lamination is used to make products such as roof beams, toys and curved pieces of furniture.

Steam Bending

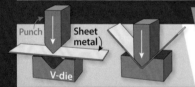

The moisture content of wood affects how pliable it is – the higher the moisture content, the easier the wood is to bend.

Steam bending is a technique that allows wood to be soaked temporarily and bent. The wood is placed in a steam box.

Once the wood has been steamed for a sufficient length of time (around an hour per 25 mm), it is bent into place around a former and clamped into position while it dries. Once dry, the wood is removed from the clamp and holds its new shape.

Line Bending

Bending Plastics

Line bending is a process used to bend thermoforming plastics such as acrylic, which cannot be bent when cold. Bending can be done using a line bender or strip heater.

A plastic sheet is heated over a strip heater. The heated strip should be positioned under the part of the sheet where the bend is required.

When the sheet is heated enough to be flexible (but not heated so much that it blisters), the sheet is carefully bent along the heated line and left to cool. Once cool, the plastic will keep its shape.

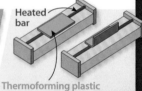

Heated bar

Thermoforming plastic

Bending Metals

Punch · Sheet metal

V-die

Metals can be bent using a wide variety of tools and machines. For example, sheet metals can be bent using a sheet metal folder, which uses punches and dies to make different bends.

Some metals are easier to work when they are heated.

Annealing involves heating a metal above its recrystallization temperature and then cooling it slowly. This alters the properties of the metal, increasing its ductility and making it more workable.

Metal becomes more stressed and prone to cracking and splitting after being bent and worked, so annealing is used to return metal to its workable form.

Pressing Metals

Sheet metals can be shaped using a stamping press, or stamping machine. A pressing die is pressed down with great force to shape the sheet. Cutting dies can also be used on these machines to pierce and cut metals.

daydream
EDUCATION

Casting

Casting is used to mould materials into shapes. Although primarily used for metals, it is also used to mould thermosetting plastics. The casting process involves pouring molten material into a shaped mould (the die) and removing it once it has cooled and solidified.

In sand casting, the mould for casting is made using a pattern (a replica of the item to be cast).

1 The pattern is placed inside a box.

2 The box is filled with moulding sand.

3 The box is then opened and the pattern is removed.

4 Molten material is poured into the cavity through specially designed channels (runners, risers and sprues) that allow air pockets to escape and the metal to flow freely.

5 The material is left to cool and solidify.

6 The box is opened, and the casting is removed.

Complicated dies can be created using CAD/CAM technology.

In the casting of plastics, a mould is filled with a liquid synthetic resin, which then hardens.

Die casting is a process that involves forcing molten metal or thermosetting plastic under high pressure into a mould cavity.

In some cases, thermosetting plastics can be cast without heating. The resin is mixed with a hardener and then poured into the cast, where it cures and hardens.

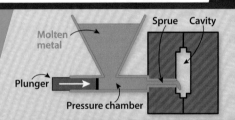

Molten metal · Sprue · Cavity · Plunger · Pressure chamber

Vacuum Forming

Vacuum forming is used to mould thermoforming plastics such as high-impact polystyrene (HIPS).

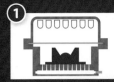
1 A plastic sheet is clamped above a mould.

2 The plastic sheet is heated causing it to become soft.

3 The vacuum bed and mould are moved up to the plastic.

4 Air is sucked out, creating a vacuum that pulls the plastic sheet onto the mould.

Once the plastic has cooled and set, the mould is lowered.

Vacuum forming is used to create various plastic products, including:

Food containers

Packaging

S
Signage

Moulding

Materials can be moulded using various processes.

Blow Moulding

Blow moulding is a process used to create hollow plastic objects, such as drinks bottles.

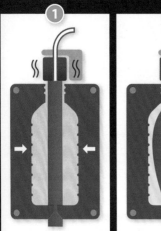

1

A parison, a softened plastic tube, is inserted into a mould.

2

Air is blown into the parison.

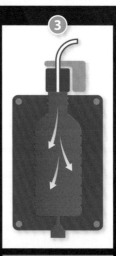

3

The parison expands to fill the mould.

4

The mould is opened to release the moulded plastic.

Injection Moulding

Injection moulding is used to create a wide range of plastic products, from model kits and dinghies to bottle tops and dustbins.

1 Plastic granules are fed into a container called a hopper and then released into an injection chamber.

2 The plastic pellets are heated in the chamber until they melt.

3 A screw in the injection chamber turns, forcing the molten plastic into the injection mould.

4 Once the plastic has cooled and set, the mould is opened to release the moulding.

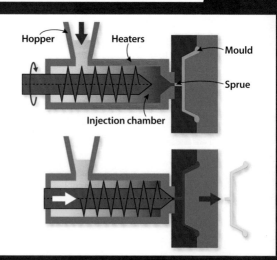

Hopper   Heaters   Mould

Sprue

Injection chamber

daydream
EDUCATION

Extrusion

Plastics and some metals, such as aluminium, can be shaped through extrusion.

Extrusion is carried out in the same way as injection moulding, but instead of filling a mould with plastic, the plastic is pushed through a die in a continuous stream.

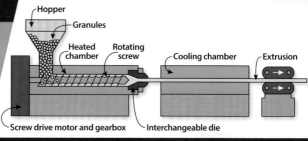

- Hopper
- Granules
- Heated chamber
- Rotating screw
- Cooling chamber
- Extrusion
- Screw drive motor and gearbox
- Interchangeable die

Extrusion is used to create the following items:

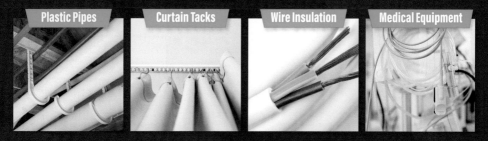

Plastic Pipes   **Curtain Tacks**   **Wire Insulation**   **Medical Equipment**

Drape Forming

Drape forming is a relatively simple process used to shape a thermoforming plastic sheet over a mould. It is used to make vehicle bumpers and curved shower screens.

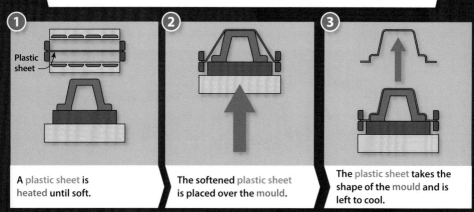

1 Plastic sheet

A plastic sheet is heated until soft.

2

The softened plastic sheet is placed over the mould.

3

The plastic sheet takes the shape of the mould and is left to cool.

Once cool, the plastic retains the shape of the mould.

Drape forming is more cost-effective than other techniques because of the low cost of tools and equipment. It also allows the material to retain its thickness, as the plastic is not stretched.

daydream
EDUCATION

Textiles: Sources & Origins

Fibres, Yarns and Fabric

Textiles are made from fibres that are spun into yarn. The yarn is then woven or knitted into fabric. Fibres can be natural (from animal or plant sources) or synthetic (man-made from chemical sources).

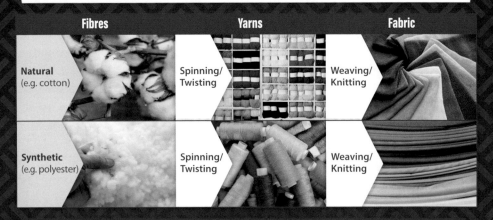

Fibres	Yarns	Fabric
Natural (e.g. cotton)	Spinning/ Twisting	Weaving/ Knitting
Synthetic (e.g. polyester)	Spinning/ Twisting	Weaving/ Knitting

There are two types of fibres: **short staple fibres** and **long filaments**.
Unlike staple fibres, filaments do not necessarily have to be spun; they can simply be twisted.
Staple fibres have a much fluffier, hairier texture than filaments, which are much smoother.

Natural Fibres

Fibres from **animal sources** are natural fibres.

Wool

Wool comes mainly from sheep, but it can also come from other hairy mammals such as goats, rabbits and camels.

The animal is sheared, and the wool is chemically cleaned and combed in a process known as **carding**.

Fibre type: Staple fibre

Silk

Silk is harvested in one continuous thread from the cocoon of the silkworm.

The cocoon is placed in boiling water to soften the sericin gum, which binds the filaments together. It is then unwound in a process known as **reeling**.

Fibre type: Filament

daydream EDUCATION

Fibres from **vegetable sources** are natural fibres.

Cotton

Cotton is a type of flowering plant found in tropical and subtropical parts of the world.

Cotton fibres grow on the ripe seedpods (**bolls**) of the plant. Once harvested, they must be separated from organic matter and cleaned before processing.

Fibre type: Staple fibre

Linen

Linen is made from the cellulose fibres found in the flax plant.

The flax is harvested 100 days after planting, and the stem is left to rot so the fibres can be retrieved. The stem is then beaten to loosen and separate the fibres before they are sorted and spun into yarn.

Fibre type: Staple fibre

Man-Made Fibres

Synthetic fibres are man-made fibres that have been created through chemical synthesis. They are polymers, or long repeating chains of molecules called monomers.

The fibres are filament fibres, so they do not necessarily have to be spun into yarn.

Examples of man-made fibres include:

Polyester

Nylon

Viscose

Lycra

Regenerated fibres come from natural sources (e.g. cellulose) that have been chemically treated.

Textiles: Properties

When textiles are selected for manufacture, it is important to consider the different properties (e.g. strength, insulation, elasticity) that make them suited to different purposes.

Sportswear

The following factors should be considered when designing sportswear:

Elasticity
Stretchy fabrics provide comfort and flexibility during physical activity. Tight-fitting garments also improve aerodynamics, which is important in sports involving speed.

Temperature Regulation
Winter sports often require clothing that keeps the performer warm. Conversely, many sports require sportswear that keeps the performer cool.

Absorbency
Many sports require fabrics that absorb very little water to keep the wearer cool. Wicking fabrics are those which draw moisture (sweat) away from the body.

Abrasion Resistance
Sportswear is often subject to a lot of wear and tear. Therefore, it needs to be hardwearing.

Elastane

Elastane is used with other materials to make stretchy fabrics, such as Lycra®. It is not very absorbent, so it helps draw moisture (sweat) away from the body.

Polyester

Polyester is often used in sportswear for its excellent wicking properties. Wicking keeps the wearer dry and cool when exercising. Polyester is also very durable.

PU Coating

Polyurethane coating is sometimes added to sports jackets and tracksuit bottoms to add waterproofing for outdoor sports. It is lightweight and flexible.

Furnishings

When purchasing furnishings, people base their decisions not only on aesthetics, but also on properties such as **durability**, **softness** and **resistance to wear**. Upholstery, for example, is available in various natural and synthetic fabrics, each with different properties.

Natural Fabrics

Cotton provides good resistance to wear, fading and 'pilling' (bobbling). This makes it durable and suitable for regular use.

Linen provides good resistance to stretching and fading. It is strong and durable but can wrinkle easily.

Synthetic Fabrics

Acrylic is often used as an alternative to wool. It is usually blended with other fibres and provides softness, insulation and good resistance to wear.

Nylon is often blended with other fabrics to give it strength. It is very lightweight and durable, making it ideal for regular use.

daydream
EDUCATION

Modification of Properties

Fabrics can have their properties modified to improve their characteristics. This can be for aesthetic and/or functional purposes.

Flame Retardants

Textile-based products that are used in the home and in public spaces can pose potential fire hazards. As a result, there are strict regulations on products such as upholstery and children's nightwear.

Fabrics can either be treated with a flame-retardant chemical or have flame resistance built into their structure to make them less prone to catching fire. However, treating fabrics with flame retardants can make the materials stiffer and weaker. Also, if a fabric has been chemically treated, the flame retardant can be washed out.

RESISTANT

Flame retardants are used in a wide variety of products, including:

Stage Drapery

Theatres and halls require fire-resistant materials, particularly if there are shows in which flames may be used.

Workwear

People who work with flames and hot materials need protective clothing to reduce the risk of burns.

Photography Backdrops

In photography studios, hot lamps are extensively used, so backdrops must be able to resist the heat.

Lamination

Layers of the same material or different materials can be sewn or bonded together to improve their physical properties, such as water resistance or stain protection.

For example, Gore-Tex® is a breathable fabric that uses layers of different materials bonded together to create a lightweight, waterproof fabric for all-weather use.

Exterior

Transpiration   Rain   Abrasion-resistant shell

Protection

Gore-Tex® membrane

Protection

Transpiration   Soft inner liner

Interior

Textiles: Stock Forms, Types & Sizes

Yarns

Yarn is available in hanks, balls and reels. Balls and hanks are generally sold by weight, whereas reels are often sold by length.

Yarn is also available in different thicknesses, or plies. For example, 2-ply wool is made up of two plied (twisted) strands, whereas 4-ply is made up of four plied strands.

Fabrics

Fabrics are generally sold in rolls of standard widths. Some common widths are 90 cm, 115 cm and 150 cm.

The length can be specified depending on individual requirements.

Standard Components

There are a range of standard components that can be used with textile-based materials, either to improve functionality or for aesthetic reasons. This includes the following fastenings.

Zips

Zips are devices used to fasten two sides of a fabric together. They can be open (like on a jacket) or closed (like on a pencil case) and can be made of metal or plastic.

Teeth – Interlock to open or close both sides of the fabric

Tape – Usually made of polyester; comes in a range of colours

Slider – Joins the teeth when open or separates them when closed

Press Studs

Press studs, or poppers, are small, round fasteners. They are pressed together to 'pop' into place and hold fabric together.

Velcro

Velcro® is a simple and quick way to fasten fabrics. It consists of two halves: one with thousands of tiny hooks and the other with tiny loops. Pressing each half together fastens the Velcro tightly.

Buttons & Toggles

Buttons and toggles are sewn onto the fabric and then fed through a buttonhole or loop to fasten the fabric.

daydream EDUCATION

Textiles: Shaping & Forming

Textiles can be cut, sewn, pleated, quilted and piped.

Cutting and Shearing

There are a range of tools available for cutting and shearing fabrics.

Fabric Shears

Also known as dressmaking scissors, these have long, sharp blades to cut fabric quickly and neatly.

Pinking Shears

These have serrated blades that are used to cut a zigzag edge into certain fabrics to stop them from fraying.

Embroidery Scissors

These have short, sharp blades that are suited to delicate work such as cutting threads. The blades are slightly curved to prevent them from piercing the fabric.

Seam Rippers

These have a small, forked blade that is used to unpick seams. The prongs help to grip tight threads so that the blade can cut them.

Craft Knives

These are used for intricate work that requires a great deal of accuracy – for example, cutting out stencils.

Rotary Cutters

These have a circular blade that is rolled across the fabric to cut through several layers at once. They are often used to accurately cut curves.

Electric Rotary Cutters

These cut in the same way as handheld rotary cutters but at a much greater speed. They are commonly used when cutting on a commercial scale.

CAM Cutting Machines

These cut designs from CAD software. They can cut through multiple layers of fabric very quickly and with great accuracy using sharp blades or lasers.

Sewing

Sewing uses stitches made with a needle and thread to permanently join fabrics and to attach objects. It can be performed by hand or with a sewing machine. There are various types of stitches, and each is suited for different purposes.

Running

This is a small even stitch that runs back and forth through the cloth without overlapping. It is used to sew basic seams.

Back

Individual stitches are made backward to the general direction of sewing. It is more durable than a running stitch.

Blanket

This stitch reinforces the edges of fabrics to prevent them from fraying. It is also used to provide a decorative finish.

Zigzag

Cross

Chain

French Knot

Seams

A seam is the join where two or more pieces of fabric meet. An unfinished seam leaves the edges open to fraying. As a result, seams are usually finished in different ways.

Plain Seam

This seam gives a neat finish with no visible stitching from the outside. The fabrics are placed together, with the outward-facing sides facing each other. Then a straight stitch is sewn slightly in from the edge of the fabrics (creating a seam allowance) to join the fabrics. The edges are then usually finished with pinking shears or a stitch.

Overlocking Seam

Overlocking seams are commonly used with stretchy and knitted fabrics. They are completed with an **overlocker**. This machine cuts off any excess seam allowance before enclosing the edges of the fabric in several threads. The end result is a neat, enclosed seam.

French Seam

French seams are ideal for fabrics that are prone to fraying. The raw edges are neatly enclosed in a strong, finished seam. French seams are used for undergarments and baby clothes to prevent the seam from rubbing against the skin.

Flat-Felled Seam
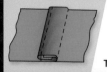

Flat-felled seams, which are commonly used for jeans and hard-wearing fabrics, involve two lines of stitching. First, stitch a plain seam to join the fabrics together. Then, trim one side of the seam allowance and wrap the untrimmed seam allowance around this. Iron the fabrics flat and add a second stitch along fold. This gives a strong and durable finish, but it can appear too bulky on finer fabrics.

daydream EDUCATION

Pleating

To create pleats, fabric is folded by doubling cloth upon itself and stitching it in place. Pleating can also be done through **heat setting**. Thermoplastic fabrics (e.g. polyester and nylon) are put into a special mould and heated to create permanent pleats.

Knife pleat

Box pleat

Inverted pleat

Pleats are used for **aesthetic purposes** (e.g. to give clothes a 'tailored' look) or for **functional purposes** (e.g. to add strength to the material or to create more space for the wearer's comfort).

Gathering

Gathering is a technique used to add fullness to a fabric by pulling it together evenly. It is commonly used in skirts and curtains.

1	2	3

Sew two straight parallel lines from one end of the fabric to the other. Do not backstitch on either end.	The ends of each row of stitching are left loose so that they can be pulled tight from both ends to gather the fabric to the desired size.	Once the size is right, the loose threads can then be knotted to keep the gathering in place. The gathered fabric can also be sewn onto another piece of fabric.

Quilting

Commonly used in bedding, quilting involves sewing **wadding** (soft material) between two layers of fabric. It traps warm air between the layers to provide insulation.

Quilting can be performed with a sewing machine or by hand. Decorative patterns are often stitched into the top layer.

Piping

Piping is a decorative trim used to finish the edges of products such as cushions or upholstery. It consists of a strip of material wrapped and sewn around a cord or folded fabric.

The strip of material is usually cut along the **bias** (i.e. diagonally through the threads of the fabric) to add flexibility. The fabric is sewn face down over the piping so that the seam is hidden when it is attached to the product.

Piping can be used to add strength and rigidity to a product as well as for aesthetic purposes.

Textiles: Surface Treatments & Finishes

Fabric surfaces can be treated and finished to enhance their functional and aesthetic properties. This can be done by hand or with specialist equipment and machines.

Dyeing

Dyes can be used to change the colour of fabrics. There are two main types of dye:

Natural dyes are derived from natural sources such as plants, insects, minerals and molluscs. They were the only dyes available before the invention of synthetic dyes.

Beetroot is used to dye and colour food, clothing and hair.

Synthetic dyes are man-made chemical compounds that have been manufactured from organic molecules. They are widely used to produce bright and consistent colours.

The first synthetic dye was mauveine, a purple dye discovered in 1856.

Dyes can be applied at various stages of the manufacturing process. Fibres and yarns can be dyed before they are spun or woven, or dyes can be applied directly to finished fabrics or garments. When dyeing fabrics, it is important to consider the following factors:

Absorbency

Highly absorbent fabrics such as cotton absorb dye easily, whereas some fabrics that are non-absorbent have to be chemically treated before being dyed to 'fix', or set, the dye.

Colour

If a dye is applied to a white fabric, it will take on the same colour as the dye. However, for a non-white fabric, the finished colour will be a mix of the dye and the natural fabric colour.

Commercial Dyeing

Commercial dyeing is used in industry to dye large volumes of fabric the same colour. This allows manufacturers to work more efficiently in terms of time and cost.

Continuous Dyeing

In continuous dyeing, yarn or fabric is fed continuously into a dye tank or bath.

After application, the dye is typically fixed with heat or chemicals and then washed.

Long rolls of fabric with a uniform colour are produced in one continuous process.

Batch Dyeing

In batch dyeing, yarn or fabric is loaded into a dyeing machine with a solution containing the dye. Because the dyes in the solution have an attraction to the fibres, the dye leaves the dye solution and enters the fibres.

The dye is fixed with heat and/or chemicals and then washed.

daydream EDUCATION

Resist Dyeing

Resist dyeing is usually performed by hand and involves using a resist, which acts as a barrier between the fabric and the dye. It is used to create patterns during the dyeing process.

Batik

Batik is a method of resist dyeing that originates from Indonesia. It uses a hot wax resist.

1  A paintbrush or tjanting tool is used to hand apply a design in hot wax. A stamp can be used for larger designs.

2  Once the wax has hardened and dried, the fabric is immersed in dye, or the dye is applied with a paintbrush.

3  The wax and dye may be applied several more times depending on the final desired effect. The fabric is left to dry each time.

4  Once the design is finished, the wax is removed by applying heat to it. This can be done by ironing or boiling it.

Batik produces unique and complex designs. Sometimes wax is also cracked for effect.

Tie-Dye

Tie-dye is a simple method of resist dyeing that uses string or elastic bands to create a barrier between the dye and the fabric. The way in which the fabric is folded and twisted can also act as a barrier.

1

The fabric is tied with string or elastic bands. Tying the fabric in different ways will produce different effects.

2

The fabric is immersed in a dye bath and then left to dry. The process can also be repeated to produce multicoloured fabric.

3

Once the tying-and-dyeing process is complete, the fabric is untied and left to dry to reveal the finished result.

Different tie-dye effects can be created by manipulating the fabric in the following ways:

- Knotting
- Folding
- Twisting
- Tying in buttons/pebbles

Printing

Printing is used to apply coloured patterns to fabrics. This can be done either by hand or with the aid of a machine.

Screen Printing

Screen printing uses stencils (designed and cut by hand or by using CAD/CAM) and a mesh screen to transfer a design onto fabric.

Screen Printing by Hand

Flatbed screen printing is a simple process that can be carried out by hand. It uses a stencil and a mesh screen to print designs on fabric.

1 The stencil is placed between the mesh screen and the fabric.

2 Ink is spread over the mesh screen using a squeegee.

3 The ink is pressed through the mesh and the holes in the stencil onto the fabric, resulting in a printed design.

Screen printing is a low-cost option for printing small runs of intricate designs, such as bespoke t-shirts or individual craft projects. However, stencils can take a long time to create, and colours have to be applied separately.

Industrial Flatbed Screen Printing

In cases where large runs of printed fabric are needed, such as in retail, machines can be used for screen printing. Although efficient, the screens can be expensive.

1 The conveyor moves the fabric under the screens.

2 The colours are applied to the fabric by automated squeegees. Each screen applies a different colour and/or pattern.

3 The printed fabric is removed ready to be fixed and dried.

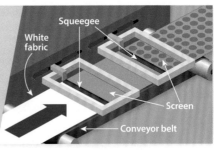

Squeegee

White fabric

Screen

Conveyor belt

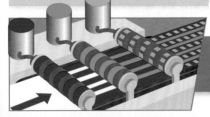

This process can also be carried out using cylinders instead of screens in a process known as rotary screen printing.

Like screen printing by hand, industrial flatbed screen printing is capable of printing intricate designs. However, it is much faster and can produce multiple designs very quickly. Unfortunately, the presses are also expensive, so it is only suitable for long runs.

daydream
EDUCATION

Block Printing and Roller Printing

In block printing, a raised design is created on a block, which is then placed in dye and pressed against fabric to transfer the design to the fabric.

For large-scale printing, roller printers can be used. These are usually engraved or embossed copper rollers that are inked and continuously run over the fabric.

Digital Printing

Digital printing uses CAD/CAM to create complex designs that are then printed directly onto fabric using inkjet technology, which can use a wide range of colours.

Digital printing is best suited to items requiring a high level of detail that are produced in small quantities.

After printing, the fabric is treated with steam or heat to fix the dye to the fabric.

Advantages

Complex designs can be produced with a high level of detail and a wide range of colours.

The process is fast compared to other methods, from design through to the finished product. Designs can therefore quickly be adapted to suit changing trends.

Disadvantages

Digital printing is a relatively new technology and is therefore costly to set up.

Ink cartridges and regular machine maintenance are also costly.

Surface Treatment

Surface treatments can be added to textiles to improve their functionality or their aesthetics. For example, they can be made crease-resistant, flame-retardant, shiny or waterproof.

After a textile-based product is made, stain resistance can be added to keep it in good condition and protect it from spillages.

This is important for use in furnishings where people often spill food or drink onto the fabric.

Stain resistance is applied to prevent water- or oil-based stains from absorbing into the fabric.

Electronic Systems: Properties

The physical and working properties of different materials make them suited for use in different electronic and mechanical systems.

Domestic Appliances

Designers need to consider the function of appliances when selecting materials. For example, an electric blender needs to be durable and waterproof to withstand repeated use and washing, but small and lightweight enough to carry and store when not in use. For this reason, a mixture of glass, plastic and sometimes stainless steel is often used.

Developments in electronic and mechanical systems have helped make domestic appliances smarter, more energy efficient, stronger and lighter.

Cordless vacuum cleaners, such as the Dyson V10, have made use of new battery technologies and stronger yet lighter materials to deliver an enhanced cleaning experience.

The development of PIC (Peripheral Interface Controllers) has also meant that devices can be programmed to perform multiple tasks and processes. This has improved the functionality and efficiency of many appliances such as washing machines, microwave ovens and central heating systems.

Motor Vehicles

In the automotive industry, it is vital that selected materials are suited to their intended function. For example, car bodies need to be made of materials that are tough to provide protection but lightweight enough for efficiency. As a result, aluminium is a popular choice.

Thanks to new technology, many vehicles now come with advanced safety features such as:

Forward Collision Mitigation

Radar is used to scan the road in front of the vehicle and alert the driver if there is a sudden reduction in the distance to the vehicle ahead.

Lane Departure Warning

A camera-based system is used to monitor the position of the vehicle in relation to lanes in the road. If the driver unintentionally strays out of the lane, the driver is alerted.

Adaptive Cruise Control

Radar is used to scan the road in front of the vehicle. The vehicle then automatically adjusts its speed to maintain a safe distance from the vehicles ahead.

Developments in renewable energy resources, recycling and new materials have led to vehicles becoming more **sustainable**. Hybrid and electric cars produce less CO_2 emissions than petrol and diesel cars, and the increased use of lightweight and recycled materials has improved efficiency and end-of-life recovery.

daydream EDUCATION

Modification of Properties

The properties of materials can be enhanced so that they can be used to perform new functions in electronic and mechanical systems.

Photo-Etching PCBs

A photoresist is a material that loses its resistance due to a chemical change when exposed to light. It is used in **photo-etching** to transfer the design of a circuit onto PCBs.

The PCB Photo-Etching Process

1 The circuit is drawn on a **mask**, usually by using CAD software.

2 The mask is placed on a copper-coated photoresist board. The parts covered by the mask will be protected from the UV light.

3 The board is exposed to UV light, which causes a chemical change.

4 The board is placed into an etching tank to remove excess copper and reveal the tracks.

Anodising Aluminium

Metals such as aluminium can be **anodised** to make them more resistant and stronger. This is done through **electrolysis**, a process that causes the surface of aluminium to oxidise.

The resulting aluminium oxide layer is dense, very hard and firmly joined to the underlying material. This protects it from corrosion and wear.

Benefits of Anodised Aluminium

- It is hard-wearing and long-lasting, extending the life of aluminium products.
- It does not peel or chip.
- It can be dyed different colours.
- It is a good electrical insulator.
- It is easily recyclable.

Uses of Anodised Aluminium

- Aircraft parts
- Electronics, such as smartphones
- Architectural features, such as cladding
- Exterior panels for spacecraft
- Vehicle parts, such as wheel covers
- Cooking pans

Electronic Systems:
Stock Forms, Types & Sizes

Electronic components are available in a wide range of shapes, sizes and quantities.

Current and Voltage

Components have current and voltage ratings that display the levels at which they are designed to work. The voltage and current ratings of a component indicate the voltage at which the appliance is designed to work and the current consumption at that voltage.

What Is Voltage?

Voltage, measured in volts (V), is the **potential difference** between two points in an electric circuit. It is provided by an energy source, such as a battery, and is needed to make current flow in a circuit.

What Is Current?

Current, measured in amperes (**amps** or **A**), is a flow of electrical charge in a circuit. It is carried by moving electrons in a wire.

| Any lower and the component may not work effectively (e.g. a buzzer may be too quiet) | ⚡ **Too low** | Current/voltage rating | ⚡⚡⚡ **Too high** | Any higher and the component could fail (e.g. a bulb could blow) |

Example

Mains power supplies typically have a power supply of 230 V. Using a component such as a small electronic buzzer, with a rating of 1.5 V, would damage the buzzer. However, mains power supplies are ideal for appliances such as kettles, which have a voltage rating very close to the power supply.

Standard Components

There are various standard components available for use within a circuit.

Dual In-Line (DIL) IC Packages

Integrated circuits (ICs) are components that can perform multiple tasks, thus reducing the number of components needed in a circuit. They are essentially mini-circuits.

A dual in-line IC package (DIL) is an IC packaged inside a block of black plastic. It has two parallel rows of tiny pins, with each pin often having a specific function.

A DIL can be attached to the circuit by soldering, but to avoid heat damage, an IC socket is often used. An IC socket also allows the DIL to be changed easily for repairs.

daydream
EDUCATION

Programmable Intelligent Computers (PICs)

A microcontroller is a type of IC that is used in a wide variety of electronic devices to perform specific tasks. It contains memory, programmable input/output peripherals and a processor, and it runs at a voltage of between 3 and 5.5 V.

PICs are a type of microcontroller.

They are available with a range of memory storage capacities, including **flash memory**, which allows PICs to be reprogrammed repeatedly so they can be used again.

PICs are ideal for a diverse range of applications (e.g. video games and household appliances) because they are low-cost, easy to reprogram and can perform multiple tasks.

Resistors

Resistors reduce or limit the current in a circuit to prevent damage to components. Resistance is measured in ohms (Ω).

Resistors come in hundreds of different values. They are coded with a series of coloured bands that identify their resistance value.

Four-band resistors have two resistance bands, one multiplier band and one tolerance band.

4-band resistor (looser tolerance)
560k Ω with ±10% tolerance

Five-band resistors have three resistance bands, one multiplier band and one tolerance band.

5-band resistor (narrower tolerance)
237 Ω with ±1% tolerance

Colour	Digit 1	Digit 2	Digit 3	Multiplier	Tolerance
Black	0	0	0	× 1 Ω	
Brown	1	1	1	× 10 Ω	± 1%
Red	2	2	2	× 100 Ω	± 2%
Orange	3	3	3	× 1k Ω	
Yellow	4	4	4	× 10k Ω	
Green	5	5	5	× 100k Ω	± 0.5%
Blue	6	6	6	× 1M Ω	± 0.25%
Violet	7	7	7	× 10M Ω	± 0.1%
Grey	8	8	8		± 0.05%
White	9	9	9		
Gold				× 0.1 Ω	± 5%
Silver				× 0.01 Ω	± 10%

Three-band resistors have no tolerance band but have a tolerance of ± 20%.

Six-band resistors have an additional band that specifies the temperature coefficient.

Instead of being produced for every possible resistance, resistors are manufactured in series. Each series has a different set of standard resistance values.

The E12 resistor series is made up of 12 different values (**1.0, 1.2, 1.5, 1.8, 2.2, 2.7, 3.3, 3.9, 4.7, 5.6, 6.8** and **8.2** Ω), each of which can be multiplied to the power of 10.

Each value has a tolerance of ±10%.

Electronic Systems: Shaping & Forming

Components in systems can be **cut**, **drilled** and **soldered**.

Cutting

Components in electronic and mechanical systems are made from a variety of materials that can be cut in different ways.

Laser Cutters

Laser cutters use high-powered lasers to cut a wide range of materials including acrylic, paper, wood and metal (e.g. stainless steel).

A laser beam is directed through a lens that focuses it down to a very small high-intensity beam. This focused beam burns through the material to provide very accurate and fine cuts, even in the smallest of components.

Advantages

- Laser cutters have a very high degree of accuracy.
- Complex designs can be created with CAD.
- Lasers do not wear with repeated use as blades do.

Disadvantages

- Laser cutting consumes a lot of energy, which makes it expensive.
- It is not suitable for all materials. For example, PVC releases toxic chlorine gas when cut.

Printed circuit boards (PCBs) can be cut using laser cutters, guillotines or utility knives.

Drilling

Drills are used to make very small holes in PCBs where components are connected. The pins or wires of the components are inserted into the holes and soldered in place.

Because of the small size of these holes (usually no more than 1.5 mm in diameter), specialist drill bits are required. Also, PCB soldering pads must be drilled completely straight, so a drill press mounted on a stand is often used for improved accuracy.

CNC milling machines can be used to mill or drill circuit boards. If a hand drill is used, specialist tools such as pin chucks are often used to make the process easier by enhancing the grip.

Laser drilling is another option. The fine laser makes it the most precise method of drilling small holes, but it is also the costliest.

Soldering

Soldering involves joining metal with a filler (usually an alloy of lead and tin) that has a relatively low melting point. The filler is melted with a soldering iron and applied to the parts that are to be joined. Soldering is used to attach components to circuit boards.

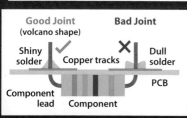

Good Joint (volcano shape)   Bad Joint

Shiny solder   ✓ Copper tracks   ✗   Dull solder

PCB

Component lead   Component

- Components are soldered into place by attaching them, their pins or wires to copper tracks or wires on the PCB.
- The solder should be 'volcano-shaped'. This can be achieved only if both the component leg and the wire or copper track is hot enough.
- Protruding wires are then snipped away after soldering.

Solder is an electrical conductor and provides a low-resistance path for current to flow from one component to another. Also, solder wire contains flux, which prevents the metals from oxidising.

Flow Soldering

Flow (or 'wave') soldering is used in large production runs to connect components to PCBs.

1 The circuit board is passed over a pan of molten solder.

2 A pump causes an upwelling of solder that looks like a wave.

3 As the PCB makes contact with this wave, the components get soldered to the board.

It is vitally important that components are assembled correctly and that any parts that do not need soldering are covered by a protective film.

Pick and Place Assembly

Components can be placed on PCBs by hand or by using a computer numerical control (CNC) **pick and place machine**.

Before pick and place machines, all placement was done manually – even for complex PCBs such as those found in TVs. Nowadays, pick and place machines offer a far more efficient and accurate method of populating PCBs ready for soldering.

Components are picked off reels or tapes with suction cups. These are then rotated to the correct angle according to preprogrammed instructions and placed on the PCB.

Although costly to set up, pick and place machines are ideal for producing complex PCBs quickly and accurately on an industrial scale. There is therefore less waste due to error.

Electronic Systems: Surface Treatments & Finishes

Surface treatments can be used to protect system components from damage caused by corrosion and friction.

PCB Lacquering

PCBs are used in many industrial and domestic items that are exposed to moisture, dust, extreme temperatures and chemicals during their use. Over time, these factors can cause corrosion.

To protect a PCB from damage, a PCB lacquer (or conformal coating) can be applied to the surface of the board in the form of sprays, paints or liquid dips. This creates a thin polymer film that acts as a protective barrier.

PCB lacquering not only improves the lifespan of the PCB, but it also makes the product more reliable.

Lacquer appears as a green-white colour under UV light. This makes it easy to inspect the thoroughness of the coating during quality control.

Lubrication

Friction is the resistance caused when two surfaces rub together. Friction can prove helpful in some applications (e.g. braking systems, grips on shoes). However, it can also cause problems in electronic and mechanical systems.

Lubrication is the process of reducing friction with oils, greases, fluids or even gases.

Oil	Grease	Graphite

This is a liquid made from long chains of polymers.	This is a liquid composed of oils and thickeners.	This is a dry lubricant that can work at higher temperatures.
Uses: hinges, bearings	**Uses:** gears, chains	**Uses:** locks, fasteners

Gears, for example, rely on smooth movement to prevent the teeth wearing away too quickly. If there is too much friction, the gear mechanism slows down. Some of the kinetic energy is therefore wasted as heat energy, making the process inefficient. The addition of a lubricant, such as oil, enables the gears to slip past each other freely with minimal friction.

Production Aids

Production aids are used to improve the speed and accuracy of production.

Reference Points

A reference point, or datum, is a point from where all measurements are taken.

In drawings, measurements are often taken from a reference line or surface. In this drawing, the vertical measurements have been taken from the bottom edge, and the horizontal measurements have been taken from the right edge.

Measuring from a reference point increases accuracy and reduces measurement error.

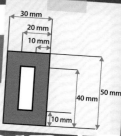

Reference points are often used to scale drawings. When using coordinates, the reference point is usually located where the axes meet (2D: 0,0 or 3D: 0,0,0).

To create a rectangle that is double the size of rectangle *ABCD*, multiply each of the coordinates of its corners by two and plot the new coordinates.

Templates, Jigs and Patterns

Templates, jigs and patterns are tools that help to improve the accuracy and consistency of repetitive designs. They are ideal for batch production because they can be used over and over again.

Templates

Templates are shapes that can be drawn or cut around to produce a specific shape. Using a template ensures that all designs are identical, and it is far quicker than drawing a design to scale every time.

Jigs

Jigs are used to guide tools. They negate the need for marking up, thus saving time, and they improve accuracy. For example, drilling jigs can ensure that holes are drilled in exactly the same place on each part.

Patterns

Patterns are templates that can be used in textiles or casting.

Textiles

Patterns are used to trace outlines onto textiles so that they can be cut out and sewn together. Tracing can be done by hand or by using CAD/CAM technology.

Casting

Patterns in casting are commonly made from metal, wood and plastic resin. A molten material is poured into the mould created by the reusable pattern to create an object that is the same shape as the pattern.

Quality Control

Quality control is used to check the quality of a product against a set standard or specification.

When customers purchase a product, they expect their needs to be met at the very least. The product has to both look right and be able to perform its expected function.

In order to ensure product quality, measurable and quantitative systems should be used at every stage during the manufacturing process.

Tolerances

Tolerance is concerned with accuracy and can be defined as the variation allowed from a precise measurement.

± 0.5 mm

The product can be within a 0.5 mm limit above or below the specified measurement.

± 0.25 g

The product can be within a 0.25 g limit above or below the specified weight.

± 5% Ω

The product can be within a 5% limit above or below the specified resistance.*

* On resistors, a 5% tolerance is represented by a gold band.

Tolerances are included on working drawings to ensure manufacturers are aware of upper and lower limits. Tolerances reduce the risk of improper fits, delays, waste and costs for replacement.

Quality Control Checks for Different Materials

When designing a product, it is important to consider what sort of checks can be used as part of quality control. Often, this depends on the materials used.

Registration Marks

The quality of colour printing can be checked by using **registration marks**.

A registration mark consists of a circle with a cross through it. To test whether all the inks in a printer are correctly aligned, all four colours are printed onto the mark.

If the printing plates are all aligned correctly, the registration mark will be clear and defined.

If the printing plates are misaligned, the registration mark will be fuzzy and colour will be visible.

daydream
EDUCATION

Go/No Go Gauges

Go/no go gauges are used to check that component dimensions are within the specified tolerances. They are often double-ended with each side manufactured to the upper and lower tolerances. The gauge is positioned onto components to ensure that they are within the accepted tolerance.

Go/no go gauges save time by eliminating the need to measure exact dimensions. They are simple, portable and require no power.

Depth Stops

Depth stops control the depth of drilling. They are fitted to the drill and set to an exact limit. When drilling a hole, the depth stop prevents the drill from going any further than the depth limit.

Depth stops are not fixed. To change the depth limit, the depth stop can simply be moved to a different position.

Laser Settings

Laser settings on laser cutters ensure that dimensions of cuts are within the specified tolerances.

Laser cutters can be programmed to cut to a very small tolerance. The **kerf** (thickness of the cut), beam focus, power and **feed rate** (speed of the cut) all need to be set correctly to produce an accurately cut product.

Checking Textile-Based Materials

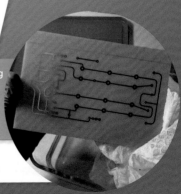

To check the quality of repeating prints on textiles, prints can be compared to the original sample. Prints must repeat correctly both vertically and horizontally. This can be checked visually by holding up the new fabric against the original and seeing how closely they match.

UV Exposure, Developing and Etching Times

Printed circuit boards (PCBs) are often manufactured by using photoetching. This requires exposing the PCB to UV light, developing solution and etching solution.

Exposure times to UV light and the time spent in the developing and etching solutions affect the amount of copper photoresist left on the PCB. Too much exposure and too much time in the solutions will remove all the copper photoresist, whereas too little may leave unwanted copper on the PCB.

Once the right time limits have been found, they should be used for every PCB produced to ensure consistency in quality.

daydream EDUCATION

Collecting & Analysing Data

Before designing a product, designers must research the wants and needs of the client or user. These can be investigated by collecting and analysing primary and secondary data.

Investigating Data

At all stages of the design process, data needs to be collected and analysed to determine the wants and needs of the **target market**. Both **primary** and **secondary data** can be used to give an insight into people's views.

Sources of Primary Data

Primary research is carried out first-hand by the researcher. New data is collected from (potential) customers, suppliers and sellers.

Examples:
- Questionnaires
- Surveys
- Focus groups
- Observations

 Advantages
- Data is up-to-date, relevant and specific.
- Data provides an insight into the market.
- Research can be tailored to the business's needs.

Disadvantages
- Research can be expensive and time-consuming.
- To be accurate, a large sample is required.

Sources of Secondary Data

Secondary research involves accessing data that already exists. Although this data has been previously collected by a third party, it can provide important market information.

Examples:
- Market research reports
- Government reports
- Newspapers and magazines

 Advantages
- Data is usually cheap and easy to access.
- Data is useful for analysing large market segments.
- Data is often already in an easy-to-interpret format.

Disadvantages
- Data is not always up-to-date and relevant.
- Data is not specific to the business.
- Data is available to all, including competitors.

Companies are likely to use a combination of both primary and secondary research methods.

Market Research

Market research is a vital part of understanding people's needs. It is also performed to identify gaps in the market, reduce business risk and inform business decisions.

It is important to know exactly which questions need to be answered and to make sure all questions are relevant and useful. Remember, focus is key!

Where would the product be sold?

What features do people most want to see?

What is the target group?

How well do similar products perform in the market?

What price would people be willing to pay?

Common market research methods include **questionnaires, interviews, focus groups, product analysis and evaluation, ergonomics** and **anthropometrics**.

daydream EDUCATION

Questionnaires and Interviews

Questionnaires and interviews are a simple way to collect answers to specific questions. The research can therefore be tailored to find out specific details about a product or the target market.

Questionnaire

This is a series of questions conducted on paper or online, often in the form of a survey. The written format and consistent questions make answers easy to compare.

Interview

This involves asking questions face-to-face or over the phone. It allows for more detailed answers, but conversation can sometimes stray off-topic. It is useful to record the interview so that responses to key questions can be reassessed.

Questions asked in questionnaires and interviews may be open or closed.

Closed Questions — These require specific answers, such as 'yes' or 'no', or answers that are measurable or expressed numerically. Answers are easy to analyse but can lack detail.

Open Questions — These involve asking people for their views and opinions. They are good for gaining in-depth responses, but it can be difficult to compare subjective opinions.

Focus Groups

A focus group consists of people brought together to share feedback on a product or idea before it is launched. It is used to gather people's opinions and observe their reactions.

This may focus on the product as a whole or on one specific aspect (e.g. aesthetics).

Advantages

- The researchers can tailor questions to find out exactly what they need to know.
- In addition to receiving verbal feedback, researchers can observe body language.
- Responses are in-depth and insightful.

Disadvantages

- Groups can be difficult to control, and conversation may stray off-topic.
- People may be influenced to agree with the majority view.
- Sample sizes are small and may not represent the target group as a whole.

Because sample sizes are usually small, it is often best to hold several focus groups to get a more accurate representation of the target market.

Product Analysis and Evaluation

Product analysis involves examining how well a product works and how well it performs in the market. Products may be investigated in terms of:

Materials used

Cost

Environmental impacts

Safety

Market opinion

Social impacts

Retail price

Manufacturing processes

Aesthetics

Functionality

Different products can be compared to judge which aspects of a product work and which do not. For example, a product's performance could be tested under certain conditions, or a product could be analysed in terms of looks, feel, smell, taste or sound. Variations of a product can also be analysed and compared.

Ergonomic and Anthropometric Data

Ergonomics is about how a person interacts with a product and their environment. It is important that users feel comfortable using a product, so a lot of research is performed before a product is released to ensure it is appealing and suitable for the target market.

Anthropometrics is the study of the measurements and proportions of the human body. In product design it involves taking measurements of people. For example:

Head circumference

Height

Waist size

Leg length

Anthropometric data is taken from a large sample of people of various shapes and sizes. It is used to determine the most likely size required by the average product user.

Example: School Chair

To make an ergonomically designed school chair, the wants and needs of the user must be considered. It must be comfortable, support the user's back and be at a height that allows the user's feet to comfortably touch the floor. It must also be sturdy and safe to use.

Suitable anthropometric data for this type of product would include height when seated, weight and hip breadth. This would be collected from a large sample of people from the target group (in this case, children aged 11–16) to find the measurements of the average user.

The product can then be designed to fit the main range of users within this group. This can be done by working out percentile ranges.

daydream
EDUCATION

Percentiles

Products need to be suitable for most of their target users. However, people come in all shapes and sizes, so there will always be small number of people who fall outside of the average range. Manufacturers usually aim to make products to suit most of the target market.

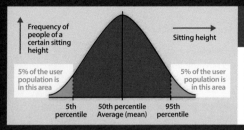

This graph shows the sitting heights of all pupils in a secondary school.

If a manufacturer were to design a chair to suit the 90% of pupils who are nearest the average sitting height, all those shorter than the 5th percentile (bottom 5%) and taller than the 95th percentile (top 5%) would not be catered for.

Presenting Data

Raw data is often difficult to understand and interpret. Because of this, it is often organised in tables, diagrams, graphs and charts that present the data in a more visual format.

Qualitative data is described using words: colour flavour sport

Quantitative data has a numerical value: age distance weight

There are two types of quantitative data:

Discrete data includes only distinct values. For example, the number of people with blue eyes can only be a whole number.

Continuous data can take an infinite number of values (within a range). For example, a person's height could be any value between 0.5 m and 2.5 m on a number line.

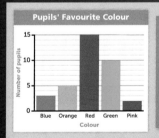

Bar charts and pie charts are great ways of presenting qualitative and discrete quantitative data.

Graphs and charts are useful for showing patterns and making comparisons.

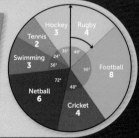

Interview transcripts can be typed in a word processing program, with important points highlighted.

Photographs and videos are used to record people interacting with a product.

Spreadsheets are a good way to present financial information, such as sales reports and forecasts.

When presenting information, include only data relevant to the investigation. This is especially important when dealing with data from focus groups.

105

The Design & Manufacturing Specifications

The main purpose of developing a new product is to solve a problem, thus satisfying a want or need. To ensure a new product is capable of this, it must go through a series of stages.

Design Brief

Once a problem or an idea has been identified, a design brief needs to be put together. This is a statement of intent that addresses how the product will solve the problem and satisfy a want or need. It also acts as a point of reference for the client and designer.

The design brief will usually contain a description of:

- Budget
- What the product should do (**function**)
- Target market
- How the product should look (**aesthetics**)
- Timescale
- Why the product is needed

The design brief can be as simple or as complex as the client wishes. However, the best design briefs have plenty of detail to inform and guide the design process. At this stage, the important thing is to outline what is needed rather than how the item will be produced.

Analysis and Market Research

Once a design brief has been created, the idea presented needs to be investigated further to improve understanding and identify any issues.

To determine if the idea is feasible, the design brief and product are analysed, and market research is performed.

Design Specification

The design specification is shaped through research and product analysis. It expands upon the design brief with specific details and ensures that the product meets its requirements.

The specification document should answer the following questions:

- How will the product work?
- What materials will be used?
- How will the design be produced?
- How much will it cost to produce?
- What are the safety requirements?

The aim of the specification is to ensure that the product meets the needs of the design brief.

Specification
Function
Target market
Durability
Size
Aesthetics
Materials
Cost
Safety
Environment
Manufacture

Having measurable specifications, such as weight and size dimensions, allows the product to be tested against the outlined requirements throughout the design process.

daydream EDUCATION

A client wants to design an educational toy laptop for children.
The design specification could outline specific requirements, such as:

Safety
The design should not involve any small parts that could come loose and pose a choking hazard.

Materials
The toy should be made of a hard-wearing polymer, that is able to withstand being dropped or handled roughly by small children.

Aesthetics
The toy should be in the shape of a small laptop with buttons that are big and easy for small hands to press as well as a touchpad. It should be available in a range of bright colours and be lightweight and compact enough to fold and carry.

Manufacturing Specification

The manufacturing specification is a document that outlines exactly how the product will be made. It often includes details such as:

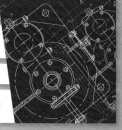

Assembly Instructions
Show how the product will be assembled and the different components attached. Diagrams such as exploded diagrams can be useful here.

Scale of Production
Shows the different production options (e.g. batch or one-off production)

Annotations
Explain important parts and features of the design

Components Required
Lists which components are needed and in what size

Tolerances
Identify the upper and lower limits of measurements

Quality Control (QC) and Assurances
Explains QC procedures and what needs to be checked

Amending the Design Brief

Product analysis and research must be performed throughout the design process to identify and solve any problems. If new information reveals flaws in the design, amendments will need to be made.

For example, during prototype development for a pair of outdoor running shoes, it could become apparent that the shoe's lightweight mesh material is not weather-resistant, which could put off some potential users. Options for alternative materials or designs may therefore need to be explored and the design specification amended.

Regular tests on designs can help identify potential issues early on. For example, a 'drop test' is used to check the toughness of children's toys that must be able to withstand rough handling.

The earlier in the design process that problems are identified, the better. Less time and money will be wasted later on in product development, when changes are likely to be costlier.

Environmental, Social & Economic Challenges

Manufacturers and designers have a responsibility to reduce the negative environmental and social impacts of new products in a way that is cost-effective and sustainable.

Climate Change

During the manufacture of many products, fossil fuels are burned for energy production and transportation. This releases greenhouse gases, such as CO_2, into the atmosphere, which many people believe causes global warming.

To reduce CO_2 emissions, designers need to consider using materials that can be manufactured with renewable energy sources and designing products that are more energy efficient.

Products can be recyclable or contain recyclable parts that are easy to disassemble at the end of the product's life.

Products that contain water (e.g. detergents) can be concentrated to reduce packaging, weight and, therefore, the energy needed for transportation.

Electronic products such as mobile laptops can be made with more energy-efficient batteries.

Deforestation

Deforestation is the clearing of rainforests and wooded areas. Trees are felled to harvest pulp and wood for paper and timber, resulting in the loss of habitats for animals.

Deforestation is also a massive contributor to **global warming**. Trees remove CO_2 from the atmosphere, so fewer trees increases levels of CO_2. The burning of wood and emissions from vehicles that transport timber also contribute to CO_2 emissions.

When sourcing materials from trees, designers can reduce the environmental impact by using:

FORESTS™ FOR ALL FOREVER
FSC
Forest Stewardship Council®

FSC-certified materials, which are sourced from sustainably managed forests

Softwoods, which take less time to regrow than hardwoods

Recycled paper or timber where possible to avoid cutting down more trees

Fair Trade

FAIRTRADE

Fair trade ensures that farmers in lower-income countries get a fair price for their produce. It also aims to improve pay and conditions for workers.

Designers and manufacturers can make their products more ethical by choosing materials produced through fair trade, but they must also consider the extra costs involved in doing so.

daydream
EDUCATION

The Work of Others

Looking at examples of work produced by other designers can inspire new designs, but they must not be copied. You will need to be familiar with the work of at least two designers and two companies listed below in preparation for your exam.

Designers

Harry Beck (1902–1974)	**Harry Beck** revolutionised how people navigate their way around cities when he redesigned the **London Underground** map. The linear and easy-to-read maps are still seen today in city transport systems worldwide.	
	Marcel Breuer was an **architect** and **furniture designer** who attended Germany's Bauhaus school of design. He is best known for his work with tubular steel furniture, such as the **Wassily chair**, as well as his bold style of architecture.	**Marcel Breuer** (1902–1981)
Coco Chanel (1883–1971)	**Coco Chanel** introduced casual but highly fashionable clothes for women through her brand, **Chanel**. The most famous of her creations include the Chanel suit, the **little black dress** and **Chanel No. 5 perfume**. The brand continues to be popular today.	
	Norman Foster is known for his striking steel and glass **architecture and design.** His most well-known creations include **Wembley Stadium**, 30 St Mary Axe (the 'Gherkin') and **City Hall** in London.	**Norman Foster** (1935–present)
Sir Alec Issigonis (1906–1988)	**Sir Alec Issigonis** was a **car designer** who was famous for introducing the British Motor Corporation's iconic **Mini** in 1959. Issigonis also designed the Morris Minor and Austin 1100. The Mini is still produced today by BMW.	
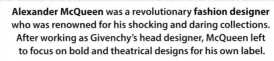	**William Morris** was a **textile designer** and leader in the **Arts and Crafts Movement.** He created works in defiance of the Victorian era's fixation on industrialisation. Many of his designs were based on nature, with flowing floral patterns.	**William Morris** (1834–1896)
Alexander McQueen (1969–2010)	**Alexander McQueen** was a revolutionary **fashion designer** who was renowned for his shocking and daring collections. After working as Givenchy's head designer, McQueen left to focus on bold and theatrical designs for his own label.	
	The **clothing and fashion designer Dame Mary Quant** combined bold colours with the Italian mod style of the era. She is renowned for popularising the **mini skirt** and was the first designer to use PVC to create **'wet look' clothing.**	**Dame Mary Quant** (1934–present)

daydream EDUCATION

Dame Vivienne
Westwood

Coco Chanel

William Morris

Dame Mary Quant

Louis Comfort
Tiffany

Philippe Starck

Ettore Sottsass

Louis Comfort Tiffany (1848–1933)	**Louis Comfort Tiffany** was an **Art Nouveau artist and designer**. He worked with ceramics, jewellery, enamel and metal. However, he was best known for his **stained glass**, particularly his intricate lamps, which are still sold today.	
	Raymond Templier came from a family of jewellers, but his work differed from their more traditional jewellery. He **designed jewellery** that was influenced by the **Art Deco movement** and his keen interest in Cubism.	**Raymond Templier** (1891–1968)
Gerrit Rietveld (1888–1964)	**Gerrit Rietveld** was a Dutch **architect and furniture designer**. He is known for his involvement in the **De Stijl** movement with artists Theo van Doesburg and Piet Mondrian. His **Red and Blue Chair** is an example of his simple, geometric style.	
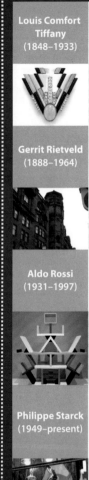	**Charles Rennie Mackintosh** was an **architect, designer and artist**. His striking **Art Nouveau style** and use of light and shade can still be seen in various buildings in Glasgow, including **The Lighthouse** and the **Glasgow School of Art**.	**Charles Rennie Mackintosh** (1868–1928)
Aldo Rossi (1931–1997)	**Aldo Rossi** was an Italian **architect and theorist** whose buildings often featured prisms, cones and cylinders. Rossi also made products for **Alessi** and wrote about architectural theory in his book *The Architecture of the City*.	
	Ettore Sottsass was an **architect and designer** who founded the **Memphis movement**, which produced post-modern products with functional designs, bright colours and unconventional shapes. He also worked as a designer for Olivetti and Alessi.	**Ettore Sottsass** (1917–2007)
Philippe Starck (1949–present)	**Philippe Starck** is a prolific **designer and architect** who started out making inflatable furniture; his works now include nightclub interiors, kitchenware and vehicles. Starck has produced designs for large companies such as Alessi, Puma and Microsoft, including the latter's optical mouse.	
	Dame Vivienne Westwood revolutionised the fashion industry in the 1970s with her unconventional **punk clothing**. She began by selling her clothing in Malcolm McLaren's London shop and continues to use traditional British materials to create **unconventional modern clothing**.	**Dame Vivienne Westwood** (1941–present)

daydream
EDUCATION

Alessi

Founded by **Giovanni Alessi** in 1921, Alessi began as a metal workshop before diversifying into **homeware products**. During the 1970s, Giovanni's eldest son Alberto took over the company and began employing leading designers to produce **bright, innovative and fun products**.

Apple

One of the most well-known brands today, **Apple** combines distinctive sleek design with an intuitive and **easy-to-use** operating system. It was founded by **Steve Jobs**, **Steve Wozniak** and **Ronald Wayne** in 1976, but the design of products such as the **iPod and Apple Watch** can be attributed to chief design officer **Sir Jonathan Ive**.

Braun

Founded in Germany in 1921 by mechanical engineer **Max Braun**, the Braun company originally produced **small radios** before branching out into **electric shavers** and **household appliances**. To this day, Braun's products are renowned for their **simple designs and usability**.

Dyson

Unhappy with traditional vacuums, **Sir James Dyson** decided a better vacuum was needed. After five years and 5,127 prototypes, he created a **bagless cleaner** that used **'cyclone technology'** to pick up dust without losing suction. With money from the sale of his early vacuums, Dyson founded his company, which now makes a range of **innovative products**.

Gap

Gap was founded in 1969 by **Doris and Donald Fisher** after Doris became frustrated that she could not find a pair of jeans that fit her. The first Gap store originally sold only **jeans** and **records** with the aim of attracting young customers. Today, Gap has five brands **selling clothing online** and in over 3,000 retail stores.

Primark

The first **Primark** store was opened by **Arthur Ryan** in Dublin in 1969 under the name of Penneys. Primark contributes to the current 'fast-fashion' trend, offering a range of **fashionable clothing at below-average prices**. Other products include homeware, footwear and beauty products. The store now operates across Europe and in the USA.

Under Armour

Under Armour was founded by **Kevin Plank** in 1996. He began the company after getting fed up with his clothes becoming wet with sweat during American Football games. His first product was a **shirt made of a lightweight material** that wicked away sweat. The company now produces a wide range of **high-quality sports apparel**.

Zara

The first **Zara** store was opened in 1975 by **Amancio Ortega**. Zara's business model is based on **high-quality but affordable fashion** that is constantly updated to keep customers returning. Zara delivers new products to stores twice weekly and produces around 12,000 designs each year! Zara now has over 2,200 stores internationally.

Design Strategies

Collaboration

Collaboration is the act of working with others to produce something. In design, this can be an invaluable way to break out of a design rut and to explore concepts that otherwise would not have been considered when working alone.

As a kitchen designer, I find it extremely useful to work with experts such as architects and interior designers. They are great for helping me to think of ideas for how to make kitchens that are practical but always very stylish.

I design toys for children aged 3–6. I like to ask a sample of children to play with the toys, and then I record how they respond to different designs. This user feedback really helps me to understand the wants and needs of my target market and enables me to collect ideas and make the necessary changes.

I am a graphic designer who mainly works with retail companies. Each brand wants to project its own image, so it is important to me to meet with clients and show them examples of designs to get feedback and ideas.

Collaboration can help at all stages of the design process, from creating prototypes, to analysing and evaluating and even after production.

User-Centred Design

User-centred design is a design strategy that puts the user at the heart of the design process. It focuses on users' wants and needs at every stage of design.

Feedback needs to be provided throughout the design process so that the designer knows exactly what works; the design is then adjusted accordingly.

Like market research, feedback may be collected via interviews, questionnaires and observations.

Systems Approach

A system is made up of parts that work together as a whole to carry out a function. Therefore, a systems approach to product design involves analysing how the different subsystems or processes in a system interact with each other to achieve the system goal. Rather than looking at how individual parts function, this approach involves analysing how the whole system works.

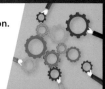

daydream
EDUCATION

Iterative Design

Iterative design is the repeated process of prototyping a design, testing it, collecting feedback, evaluating the design and making improvements based on the results. The process is repeated in a cyclical manner until the final design is ready to be produced.

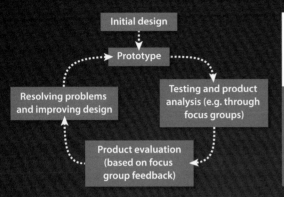

Initial design → Prototype → Testing and product analysis (e.g. through focus groups) → Product evaluation (based on focus group feedback) → Resolving problems and improving design

The repetitive nature of the iterative design process is useful for spotting problems early on and addressing them right away.

This saves on both the costs and time involved with making big changes further down the line.

Another benefit of the iterative design method is the quality feedback that is collected. This is extremely useful for making sure that product users' wants and needs are met.

Avoiding Design Fixation

Design fixation simply means getting stuck on a particular design idea. It prevents designers from exploring ideas that may be very different but much better than the original. Design fixation can happen for several reasons, including:

- Time constraints
- Low budget
- Fear of taking risks
- Pushy clients
- Being too influenced by previous successful designs

Fortunately, there are various ways in which design fixation can be overcome:

Make Small Changes

Even minor changes, such as changing the size, can be a starting point.

Collaborate

Working with others to peer review ideas and create mind maps can boost creativity.

Make a Model

Sometimes it is less constraining to just start making rather than thinking.

Developing Design Ideas

Designers can explore and develop ideas by using an iterative process, which includes sketching, modelling, testing and evaluating. An iterative process involving these steps helps designers to explore different design ideas, how well they work and how they can be improved.

Sketching

Sketching is a great way of getting initial design ideas down on paper quickly.

Rough freehand sketches are excellent for the initial brainstorming process. They can later be tidied up to present to others. More detailed sketches can be made for advanced designs and to specify particular details, such as product dimensions and materials.

Modelling

Modelling involves making simplified versions of the design that can be tested against the design specification to see if the basic design concept is likely to work. Models should ideally be made of low-cost materials that are similar to the materials intended for use in the final design.

Card Models

Card models are a quick and low-cost way to see how the shape and proportions of a product will look.

Toiles

Materials such as calico are often used to make toiles (working models of textile designs). They can be easily drawn on to mark up changes.

Breadboard

Breadboards are used to create models of electronic circuits. Components can be easily changed to create different circuits.

Computer-aided design (CAD) can also be used for modelling.

The model is digitally created in detail and viewed from any angle. CAD allows for extensive and accurate testing under various specific conditions, such as air pressure or temperature.

Testing and Evaluating

Sketches and models must be tested to check how closely the design meets the design specification. Testing allows the designer to see which aspects of the design work well and which need further work.

Once testing has been completed, the results should be evaluated and modifications to the design considered based on the results.

The sketching/modelling, testing and evaluation process is repeated until the design meets all the criteria in the design specification. Once this stage has been reached, a prototype (early working version of the final design) can be created.

daydream EDUCATION

Communication of Design Ideas

A range of techniques are used to develop, communicate, record and justify design ideas.

Freehand Sketching

A freehand sketch is performed without the use of drawing aids. It can be used to record initial designs, either in 2D or 3D, but it is most useful to include both.

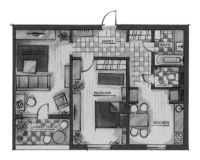

2D sketching is good for capturing dimensions.

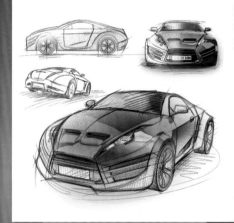

3D sketching is used to express overall shape.

Freehand sketching is the quickest method of illustration. Colour and shading can be used to represent light and shade, depth, texture and finish, whilst annotations help explain features and materials used. However, freehand sketching is not very accurate.

Isometric Drawing

Drawings constructed using isometric projection use vertical lines and lines drawn at 30° to the horizontal. A set square with a 30° angle is often used to make sure that the drawing is accurate. Isometric grid paper can also be used.

Isometric drawings provide a more realistic representation of an object than freehand drawings, but they do not show perspective.

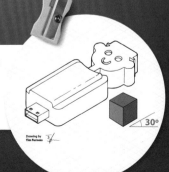

Drawing by
Tim Furness

Perspective Drawing

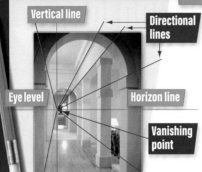

Vertical line

Directional lines

Eye level

Horizon line

Vanishing point

Perspective drawings provide a realistic representation of how objects are seen. As in real life, the further into the distance an object is, the smaller it appears.

If you stand at one end of a corridor and look down it, you will notice the walls and ceiling appear to converge (meet at a point).

The horizontal, vertical and directional lines can be extended back but will always meet at the vanishing point, which is on the horizon line.

Vanishing Point	All lines converge at this point.	**Horizon Line**	The vanishing point always appears on this line, which represents eye level.

One-Point Perspective

One-point perspective shows an object as it appears directly in front of the viewer.

There is one vanishing point on the horizon line, and all direction lines lead to this vanishing point.

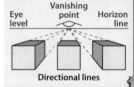

Eye level · Vanishing point · Horizon line · Directional lines

Two-Point Perspective

Drawing by Tim Fennear

Two-point perspective shows an object from a leading edge, providing a more realistic view than a one-point perspective drawing.

There are two vanishing points on the horizon line, and all direction lines lead to the vanishing points.

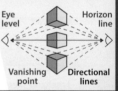

Eye level · Horizon line · Vanishing point · Directional lines

Systems Diagrams

A systems diagram is used to show how a system will work by breaking it down into basic blocks of inputs, processes and outputs.

Input

A button connected to the doorbell buzzer is pressed.

Process

An electrical signal is transmitted to the buzzer.

Output

The doorbell buzzer makes a sound.

Systems diagrams do not need to be detailed; they need to give only a very basic idea of what the system will do at each stage and the components that are required.

Schematic Diagrams

Schematic diagrams use symbols to show the layout of electrical and mechanical systems.

Schematic diagrams aim to show simply which components (represented by symbols) are used and how they are connected; they are not drawn to scale. A diagram serves as a guideline for building the system.

A circuit diagram is an example of a schematic diagram.

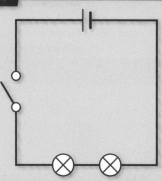

Annotated Drawings

Annotations are used to describe, explain or specify certain aspects of a design. For example, labels can be added to show sizes, materials, processes, weights and tolerances.

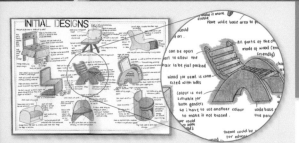

Annotations can communicate in simple terms the designer's view about a certain aspect of the design. They can also be used to note how the design fulfils criteria within the specification.

Annotations show good use of planning, decision-making and development in the design process.

Exploded Diagrams

Exploded diagrams are used to show how parts of a product fit together. They are often used in manufacturer's instructions and flat-pack furniture.

The components in the diagram are displayed separately from each other as though they have 'exploded' from the centre of the diagram. Part sizes are shown in proportion to each other.

The benefit of this is that it clearly shows which parts fit together, even if they are normally hidden in the assembled product.

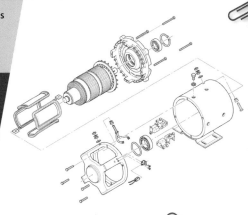

117

Orthographic projection is used to depict 3D objects as a set of 2D drawings. It shows the **front view**, **plan view** and **end view** drawn to scale, and measurements are given in millimetres.

A third angle orthographic projection is shown below.

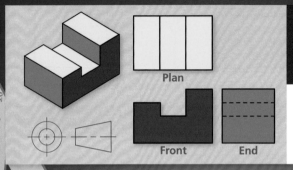

Plan

Front   End

The plan view is drawn at the top, the front view is directly below this and the end view is positioned next to the front view.

Orthographic drawings are often used in manufacturing because they provide detailed information about the design.

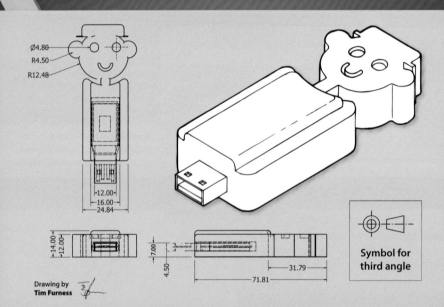

Ø4.80
R4.50
R12.48

12.00
16.00
24.84

14.00
12.00

7.00
4.50

31.79

71.81

Symbol for third angle

Drawing by
Tim Furness

Orthographic Drawing Conventions

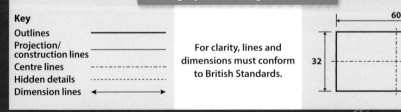

Key

Outlines	
Projection/ construction lines	
Centre lines	
Hidden details	
Dimension lines	

For clarity, lines and dimensions must conform to British Standards.

60

32

Scale and Dimensions

Orthographic projections must be drawn to scale and contain the correct dimensions.

Scale is the ratio between a drawing and the actual size of the object it shows. The scale of a drawing should be listed in the title block.

2:1 = The drawing is twice the size of the actual object.

1:1 = The drawing is to actual size.

1:2 = The drawing is half the size of the actual object.

Example

0   50 cm

Scale 1:50

The plan of Oliver's bedroom is drawn at a scale of **1:50**. This means that the bedroom is 50 times bigger in real life than in the drawing.

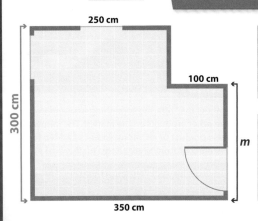

To identify the length of **300 cm** on the drawing, divide the real-life measurement by the scale:

300 cm ÷ 50 = 6 cm

To identify the length of *m* in real life, use a ruler to measure the length of *m* on the drawing (in this case 4 cm) and multiply it by the scale:

4 cm × 50 = 200 cm

Dimensions show the specific measurements of the object being drawn. They should be the actual sizes and not the scaled sizes. Measurements should be stated in **millimetres (mm)** and positioned centrally above the dimension lines.

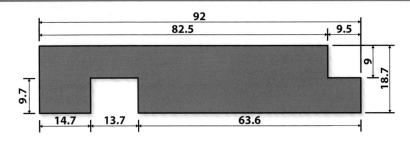

Note: The dimensions should not be written inside the object.

Prototype Development

A prototype is a pre-production working model of a product that is used to test a concept.

Prototypes are designed and developed in response to client wants and needs. They are fully functioning products or systems that allow a design to be tested and amended before the final design is created. Prototypes are usually manufactured by using the same processes as the intended final design; this ensures that both the product and the manufacturing process meet expectations.

Satisfying the Requirements of the Brief

The design brief is a point of reference for both the designer and client. It is important to refer to it when creating prototypes as a reminder of the client's specific wants and needs.

A prototype should match the criteria laid out in the manufacturing specification. Should any problems arise, they must be resolved, and the specification updated to reflect any changes.

Demonstrating Innovation

A prototype should be innovative, offering something new and exciting that differentiates it from other products on the market. The innovation could be a completely new product or an improvement or added feature that makes the product stand out from similar items on the market.

The most marketable products are usually the most innovative.

Functionality

A prototype should demonstrate that the final product will be fit for its intended purpose. To show this, a prototype needs to be tested thoroughly to ensure that it performs its function effectively.

For example, an appliance such as a toaster should be able to perform all the tasks specified in the product specification (e.g. toasting the bread and automatically popping the toast according to the adjustable settings), meet product safety regulations and withstand wear and tear.

Aesthetics

Products not only need to function well, but they should also look good.

For example, imagine big, strong hinges that fix to the outside of kitchen cupboard doors. They may function well, but they would not fit in with the design of a kitchen. A better option would be to use internal concealed hinges.

Products that look good are far more likely to be marketable. Feedback from clients and focus groups can be helpful when looking at the aesthetics of a product.

daydream EDUCATION

Marketability

A product should be **marketable** – in other words, it should offer something that makes customers want to buy it. If the product is functional, innovative and looks good, then it should appeal to the target market.

One way to test this is to present the prototype to a focus group for the target market or to conduct a customer survey questionnaire.

Evaluating Prototypes

Prototypes must go through rigorous testing and analysis to ensure they are safe, fit for purpose and meet the criteria set out in the product and manufacturing specifications. Any issues that are found need to be resolved, resulting in amendments to the design or manufacturing process.

Feedback

Gaining feedback on a prototype from the client and a sample of the target market gives designers an insight into which elements of the design work and which do not.

Feedback may flag up potential problems or potential improvements. Any changes will need to be updated and justified in the specification.

Selecting Materials and Components

The materials and components selected for use in a prototype must be cost-effective, appropriate for the intended function and readily available.

Aesthetics are also important when considering different materials and components, as customers want to buy products that look good.

A designer may consider the following questions:

- Does this material allow the product to carry out its function properly?

- Does the cost of the material stay within budget when making several prototypes?

- Are components available in stock sizes?

- Are the materials and components safe?

- Do the materials and components reflect the quality of the intended product?

- Does the material look good? What colours and styles are available?

- Is the material easy to work?

- Are the materials renewable and easy to extract?

Different materials and components can be tested in the prototyping stage until the most suitable ones are found.

Material Management

Managing materials efficiently can help to minimise waste, thus reducing the cost of materials and energy used during the manufacturing process.

Planning, Cutting and Shaping

Effective planning is key to minimising waste when cutting and shaping materials.

When cutting shapes from a material, try to determine the best way to organise the shapes so that as many as possible can be cut from the least amount of material.

The following methods are used to organise shapes as efficiently as possible.

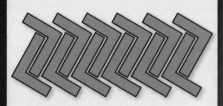

Nesting is used to arrange shapes efficiently on a piece of material by bringing the shapes as close together as possible. This reduces the amount of material wasted between each shape.

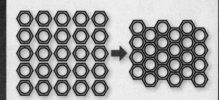

Tessellation is used for shapes that can fit perfectly together with no space between them. Waste material is kept only to the edges.

The following calculation can be used to determine the amount of waste generated by an arrangement of shapes on a material:

Wastage = Total area of material – Area of material used for shapes

Jack is making a box out of plywood. The total area required for the box is 5,400 cm. How much wastage will there be from a ply sheet measuring 60.6 × 122 cm?

Wastage = Total area of material – Area of material used for shapes

= (60.6 × 122) – 5,400

= 7,393.2 – 5,400

= 1,993.2 cm²

Remember: When taking these measurements, millimetres (mm) can offer the greatest accuracy without the need for decimal points. Keeping to this unit will also reduce any confusion caused by using different SI units.

Alternatively, CAD/CAM provides an accurate way to arrange shapes efficiently.

daydream EDUCATION

Marking Out

Accurately marking out materials ensures that they will be cut, drilled and assembled in the right place. Also, it minimises waste due to inaccuracies. It is always best to measure twice to check; use a steel ruler for lengths and a combination square for angles.

There are a variety of tools available for marking out on different materials.

Marking Tools

Try Square
Marks out and checks for 90° angles

Scriber
Scratches marks into metal and plastic

Combination Square
A multipurpose tool, often used to measure and mark out angles

Engineer's Blue
A blue dye added to metal to reveal scribe marks

Marking Knife
Scores lines in wood and some other materials

Engineer's Dividers
Marks out circles or curves on metal

Marking Gauge
Marks lines in wood that are parallel to an edge

Sliding Bevel
Marks out a required angle

Tailor's Chalk
Marks out on fabric and can be erased later on

Centre Punch
Marks out a point for drilling on metal

Templates, jigs and **patterns** can also be used to mark out repeated shapes. This is especially useful where the same shape must be repeated accurately.

When marking up and measuring is complete, cutting should ideally be done on the waste side of the line. This reduces the likelihood of the material being cut too small and having to be redone.

Additional material may be required when cutting **joints** for wood and metal. This allows the material to overlap.

Extra material may also be needed for fabrics where a **seam allowance** is needed (e.g. when sewing a plain seam).

Health & Safety

Design & Technology involves a lot of practical work, some of which involves significant risks. Therefore, it is vital to implement safe working practices to ensure a positive health and safety culture.

Risk Assessment

Before starting a new project, a risk assessment should be carried out to identify and minimise risk. A school must undertake a risk assessment for all equipment, processes and materials it uses.

Record details of any incidents, including the cause, and determine how it can be prevented in the future.

Safety in the Workshop

Rooms must be clean, tidy and in a safe condition.

Workstations should be clean and clear of excess materials and tools. After use, tools and materials should be stored correctly, with blades and sharp edges protected. Floors should be clear of obstructions and trip hazards, such as bags and scrap off-cuts.

Clothing and Protective Equipment

Ensure you have no loose clothing; tie back long hair; remove loose jewellery; and tuck in ties and apron strings.

Hazardous materials: Wear an apron or overalls, goggles and the correct gloves.
Hot materials: Wear an apron and the correct gloves; a face shield is required for some jobs.
Dust: Wear a face mask and safety goggles. Ensure there is adequate extraction.

Machine Tools

Do not use machine tools without permission or training. It is important to understand:
- The design of the machine and the names of the main parts
- How to set up the machine and use guards, running speeds and cutter settings
- How to use the machine safely (learn where the emergency stop button is located.)

Keep machines and guards clean and in good condition, and never touch moving parts. If a machine has a dust extractor, ensure it is running when in use.

Hand Tools

Perform practical work standing up and ensure materials are held securely in place using the appropriate holding device, usually a vice or a clamp. Use the correct tools and technique for the job and materials used.

Carry tools with their cutting edges pointing down, and return them to their racks when not in use.

Handling Materials and Waste

Wear the correct type of gloves when handling hot and hazardous materials. For example, wear leather for hot materials and plastic for chemicals. Only use hazardous materials where necessary, and avoid excess contact with toxic substances. Check the regulations for ventilation, and always wear safety glasses or goggles.

Dispose of waste correctly, and wash your hands after work.

Think About Safety!

Always listen to instructions and concentrate on what you are doing. Carelessness causes accidents. If you are not sure about something, ask!

daydream
EDUCATION

Notes

Notes

Index

Index

Index